21
DAYS TO

Become a
Money
Magnet

Also in the 21 Days series

21
DAYS TO

Become a
Money
Magnet

Attract Wealth, Find Abundance, and

Take Control of Your Finances

MARIE-CLAIRE CARLYLE

HAY HOUSE

Carlsbad, California • New York City
London • Sydney • New Delhi

Published in the United Kingdom by:
Hay House UK Ltd, The Sixth Floor, Watson House,
54 Baker Street, London W1U 7BU
Tel: +44 (0)20 3927 7290; www.hayhouse.co.uk

Published in the United States of America by:
Hay House Inc., PO Box 5100, Carlsbad, CA 92018-5100
Tel: (1) 760 431 7695 or (800) 654 5126; www.hayhouse.com

Published in Australia by:
Hay House Australia Pty Ltd, 18/36 Ralph St, Alexandria NSW 2015
Tel: (61) 2 9669 4299; www.hayhouse.com.au

Published in India by:
Hay House Publishers India, Muskaan Complex,
Plot No.3, B-2, Vasant Kunj, New Delhi 110 070
Tel: (91) 11 4176 1620; www.hayhouse.co.in

A catalogue record for this book is available from the British Library.

Tradepaper ISBN: 978-1-4019-7187-8
E-book ISBN: 978-1-78817-924-9
Audiobook ISBN: 978-1-78817-860-0

10 9 8 7 6 5 4 3 2 1

Printed in the United States of America

Contents

Publisher's Note

Research has shown that establishing a habit requires 21 days' practice. That's why Hay House has decided to adapt the work of some of its most prestigious authors into these short, 21-day courses, designed specifically to develop new mastery of subjects such as becoming a money magnet.

21 Days to Become a Money Magnet draws from Marie-Claire Carlyle's best-selling *How to Become a Money Magnet* (Hay House, 2010)

Other titles that will help you to further explore the concepts featured in the 21-day program are at the beginning of this book.

Author's Note

Many of the exercises in the chapters that follow need to be done on paper, so I recommend that you keep a pad of paper or a notebook and a pen or a pencil handy as you use this book.

Introduction

Thank you for choosing this book. Congratulations, too, on acknowledging your desire for more money and your intention to change your reality.

In an era when the "greedy" are receiving their comeuppance and when doing things "just for the money" is no longer acceptable, it is easy to believe that money is a dirty word. When we believe that money is a dirty word, we shy away from it and, in so doing, we turn our backs on our full potential.

This book is about how money is simply a reflection of our value, both our self-value and the value that we are providing to others.

You have found this book because you have no doubt reached a point where "enough is enough"! You are ready to take full responsibility for the amount of money you attract. You recognize a true desire for more money in your bank account and you are ready to do something different in order to change your financial circumstances, *now!*

In taking the first step and reading this book you are sending a clear sign to your subconscious that you are ready for significant change in your life. You are ready to welcome in wealth. You are ready to be truly happy.

If you have already read some books on money management, abundance, or the Law of Attraction, and nothing has changed in your financial status, don't worry. Relax.

Everyone has a turning point, a "breakthrough moment," and having watched so many people find it on the "How to Become a Money Magnet!" workshops, I have every reason to anticipate a shift in your fortunes as a result of this book. Mind you, the book does work best when you follow my suggestions!

This book has been written in an ordered sequence, starting with the theory of how to become a Money Magnet and looking at your current circumstances. Next, we investigate how you can start to attract more money into your life immediately, by following some basic steps. Then we lay the foundation required for you to become a lifelong Money Magnet.

It's best to read the book in the order it was written, and you will receive maximum benefit if you make time to do the exercises as they arise. The original "How to Become a Money Magnet!" workshop worked because the participants did all the exercises.

Throughout the book you will discover some repetition. This is intentional. It is part of the process of transforming you into a Money Magnet!

Congratulations again on reading this book. It's the first step in taking responsibility for the amount of money you attract into your life.

The money is already there. The only thing preventing you from being rich is *you*.

DAY 1

What Do We Mean By "Money Magnet"?

We are going to start today by exploring what we mean by the term "Money Magnet."

Attracting money can be incredibly easy. There are basically two main steps: understanding the scientific theory, then applying it to your own circumstances. (OK, it's not quite that simple, but you still need to know the theory!)

Have you ever noticed how some people always seem to "fall on their feet," while others have a different complaint each week? Have you noticed how people with money find it easy to attract more, while people with little money seem to get less? Have you noticed that when you feel happy, good things start to happen to you? Have you ever had a morning where you wake up late, miss your train, and spill your coffee on your new white shirt… and you just "know" that you're going to have a bad day?

These are all examples of the Law of Attraction at work. Just like the law of gravity, the Law of Attraction is a natural law of our universe, and so there is no escaping it. The Law of Attraction states "like attracts like." If you are feeling grumpy, you will attract more reasons to be grumpy. If you are celebrating some good news, you will attract more good news. If you are feeling rich and grateful for all that you have, you will attract more reasons to feel rich and grateful for all that you have.

You are already a magnet, attracting whatever you think about into your life. If you are worrying about the size of the bills you have to pay or whether you can afford to go on vacation this year, you will attract more reasons to worry. Money is likely to become more of a problem. If you feel that life is unfair, it will be unfair.

The good news is that once you understand the very simple Law of Attraction, you understand how you can attract more good things into your life.

By thinking happy and grateful thoughts, you will attract reasons to be happy and grateful. To be rich, you need to *feel* rich.

In other words, to attract more wealth into your life, you need to be giving off the "vibe" of a wealthy person… and no, this doesn't mean going to buy the latest smart TV on your credit card!

At this point, you may be tempted to buy a lottery ticket and spend the rest of the week with a big smile on your face as you practice feeling rich. (Don't worry – this is what most people are tempted to do when they first encounter the Law of Attraction.) Unfortunately, you are unlikely to win the lottery. This is because more than 80 per cent of your thoughts are subconscious, and most people have an ingrained limiting belief system about winning lotteries. We will look at limiting beliefs later on in this book.

In order to be a Money Magnet, your thoughts and feelings need to be both consciously and unconsciously aligned to the belief that you easily attract money.

Rather than focusing on *how* you will attract money, for example via a big lottery win, it is wiser to focus on feeling wealthy within yourself. Allow yourself to attract money from wherever is easiest for it to reach you. Feeling wealthy within means having high self-esteem and knowing that you are worthy of wealth.

Being a Money Magnet means finding your "inner wealth" in order to attract your "outer wealth."

Quantum Physics

So how does the Law of Attraction work from a scientific point of view? Just how are your thoughts affecting your reality? Quantum physics provides us with the answers.

You may be familiar with Einstein's equation $E=mc^2$. Quantum physics explains Einstein's theory by telling us that all matter is made up of energy. The chair you're sitting on, the drapes or blinds on the windows, your clothes, your hands, even your thoughts, are all made up of energy.

Remember when you were at school in the biology lab and you got to look through the microscope? Wasn't it amazing how an inanimate object suddenly appeared to be made up of moving cells? Well, in the same way, objects that look solid to our naked eye are actually made up of pure energy vibrating at a certain frequency. The more solid an object is, the lower its frequency of energy. As Lynne McTaggart explains in *The Field*:

> *The Einstein equation $E=mc^2$ was simply a recipe for the amount of energy necessary to create the appearance of mass. It means that there aren't two fundamental physical entities—something material and another immaterial—but only one: energy.*
>
> *Everything in your world, anything you hold in your hand, no matter how dense, how heavy, how large, on its most fundamental level boils down to a collection of electric charges interacting with a background sea of electromagnetic drag force.*

You Are an Energetic Being

Extend the concept that all matter is effectively a charge of energy and we realize that we too are, in effect, energetic beings. We are energetically connected to everything else. Let's look at some evidence of this.

Kirlian photography shows the existence of colored energy within and extending outward from a person. It is often referred to as a person's aura. Some people can actually see the different-colored auras projected by each person.

If you'd like to see your energetic field, most Mind–Body–Spirit fairs will have someone who can take an aura photograph of you. I recommend that you think happy thoughts beforehand!

Not all of us actually see auras, but most of us sense others' auras as soon as we come into their presence. Think of a person you've met and liked recently. Before you talked with each other, you may have already had a strong feeling that you were going to like this person. Conversely, you may have encountered someone recently who made you want to distance yourself as quickly as possible. These are examples of you "tuning in" to other people's energy fields and even into the pattern of their thoughts. We all do it, and sometimes we describe it as having "a gut feeling" about someone.

Once we understand that our thoughts are energetic threads that can be "received" by others, it starts to open up a whole new realm of possibility.

Have you ever thought of someone, and seconds later you receive a telephone call from that person? Or you go shopping for a friend's birthday and a certain book falls off the shelf in the shop and you realize that you've found the perfect gift?

When we use our energy to think of someone, we create the possibility of seeing them. It is as though our thought has left an imprint in the space, which now holds the possibility of it being created. It may take more than just a thought to create the possibility—after all, if the person lives on the other side of the world, it might take a video link or a plane ticket—but the possibility is there as a result of the thought.

This space is where you will find the possibility of becoming a Money Magnet.

The money is already there. The only thing preventing you from being rich is *you*.

DAY 2

How Your Thoughts Can Attract Money

Today we are going to further explore how our thoughts shape the reality of our life.

Even if we can't fully explain it, many of us will reach a point where we understand that there are connections between everything. There are just too many coincidences happening to ignore the possibility of interconnectedness.

Let's look at a simple example of interconnectedness. When I decided that I wanted a convertible car with a hardtop roof, even though at the time I didn't know that such a car existed, I was then "connected" to the newly launched Mercedes SLK. Out of all the different car models on the market, I "came across" exactly what I was looking for: a convertible with a hardtop roof that went down with the press of a button. Nowadays there are many such models on the road, but at some point a creator had the idea of such a car. He or she connected with the possibility of creating it. Customers like myself connected with the idea of owning such a car, and a new whole new market for the hardtop convertible was born.

Interconnectedness is an exciting concept. It opens up all sorts of possibilities. It makes way for the possibility of miracles. If you are vibrating at a certain frequency, then you will attract the corresponding connection. If you believe in every cell of your body that something is possible, you will connect with that very possibility. Interconnectedness means that nothing happens by accident. We have the chance to be masters of our own lives.

Living in a Realm of Possibilities

Sometimes when we learn something new, it simply raises more questions for us. For example, where did the creator of the hardtop convertible find his or her inspiration? How did the Wright brothers conceive the idea and belief that they could fly in an airplane? Where did Mozart find his music? And if we are all energetic beings swimming in a soup of energetic objects, what is this soup that connects us?

Lynne McTaggart, in *The Field*, refers to the soup as the "Zero Point." The Zero Point is described as "an ocean of microscopic vibrations, which appear to connect everything in the universe like some invisible web." The universe is described in her book as being in a state of infinite possibility. It is the consciousness of the observer that brings an observed object into being. In fact, nothing exists independent of our perception of it. In other words, every minute of every day we are creating our own reality through the concept of interconnectedness.

Bob Proctor, author of *Born Rich* and star of the film *The Secret*, refers to the connecting soup as the "formless original substance."

Both Bob Proctor and Lynne McTaggart agree that you are the creator of your world. You have created your current circumstances and you can create new possibilities for yourself.

I like to think of the connecting soup as a space for creation. It offers us the chance of a new possibility. It is where we can create those new energetic possibilities for ourselves.

If everything is connected energetically and your thoughts hold the power of creation, then you are the main creator of your world. Look around you. Look at your life. Look at how much money you have. What you have in your life is the direct result of your thoughts, whether conscious or subconscious.

Money Mastery

Understanding that you are the master of your life is the secret to attracting whatever you wish. Mastering your thoughts means choosing a direction for your life and keeping your thoughts aligned to that direction. Align your thoughts to attracting more money and you will attract more money. Focus on how little money you have and you will attract even less.

Look at your life and how it is right now. It is the result of your thoughts. If your thoughts are focused on a lack of money, this is what you will attract.

If you are tempted to blame your misfortune on others or on circumstances, such as redundancy, divorce, or illness, think again. You are falling into the temptation of playing the "victim." When we play the victim—for example, by saying "But I was made redundant!"—we surrender our power.

It is a tempting role because as the victim we avoid all responsibility. We may even gain sympathy from others.

Are You a "Poor Me" or a "Lucky Me"?

I'd now like you to take a moment to assess your own attitude to life by asking yourself the following questions.

- Is your glass half-full or half-empty?

- Are you saving for a rainy day or for an unexpected vacation?

- Do you love your job or is it just a way to pay the bills?

- Is your financial situation all the fault of someone else or are you proud of what you have achieved?

- Do you hold regrets or are you happy for the learning experiences?

- Is it "all their fault" or were you steering your own ship?

- Is it all down to the recession or to your own personal choices?

- Are you destined to continue as you are or do you see new opportunity around every corner?

- Are you accepting the news of the day or do you have your own vision of the world?

- How do you feel when it's raining? Pleased for the plants or miserable because you forgot your umbrella?

Your answers to the above questions will give you an idea of how much responsibility you take for the current circumstances of your life.

It's vital to realize that you, and you alone, are responsible for your life. Avoid the victim trap. Resolve to take responsibility for what is in your life. Resolve to shift your focus from a sense of "lack" to a feeling of richness. If there is anything you don't like in your life, for example insufficient funds in your bank account, then let's start changing that *now*!

Unconscious Thoughts

Once you acknowledge your creator role in the energetic pool of your life, everything gets so much easier. Of course, one of the challenges is that the bulk of our thoughts are actually made unconsciously. In order to breathe or to digest our food, we have to have the thought first to create the action. It's just that in the case of breathing, for example, we are unaware of the thought. It happens unconsciously.

As previously mentioned, more than 80 percent of our thoughts are unconscious, so we may be creating, unconsciously, a reality that we don't consciously like.

For example, we want to have lots of money (conscious thought), but maybe we don't actually like rich people (unconscious thought) because at a young age we learned how a wealthy ruler was mean to his people and we then concluded that all wealthy people use their power to be mean to the good people who are poor (unconscious thought).

At some level we will now protect ourselves from being wealthy and mean (unconscious thought) and we may aspire to be poor and good (unconscious thought). Conversely, we may create wealth because we think that, by becoming rich, no one can be mean to us.

Many of us look to wealth for security, and we then create just enough wealth to be secure and have our basic needs met. To have more and to be rich are considered by our unconscious to be "bad."

Clearly, the secret is to change your thoughts (conscious and unconscious) in order to create a new possibility for the amount of money in your life. We will look at the proven ways of doing this later in the book.

The money is already there. The only thing preventing you from being rich is *you*.

DAY 3

How Do You Feel About Money? (Part 1)

Yesterday you learned how your thoughts have a direct influence on your circumstances. Today we are going to explore how you currently feel about money.

It's a good idea to be in a safe, quiet place as you read this chapter. This is your opportunity to really get to the heart of what has been holding you back.

You may think that you wish to be rich, but deep down you may feel that being rich is an unsafe place to be. You may have an opinion that rich people can attract jealousy, theft, disloyalty, and superficial friends. Maybe it feels much safer for you to stay within a certain income level, where you are less exposed to potential attack. The word "money" can provoke quite extreme reactions in some people. Many people see a straight choice between being poor and spiritual or being rich and selfish. They flinch at the very mention of "money." It is seen as a dirty and even vulgar subject. I received some of this type of negative feedback on first launching my "How to Become a Money Magnet!" workshops.

When I'm delivering a workshop or a talk on becoming a Money Magnet, I often start by congratulating the audience for publicly declaring their desire for more money. After all, if you cannot happily admit to yourself that you wish to be a Money Magnet, you will have a long way to go before you start to attract more money.

Money Is an Emotional Subject

As we are delving into the emotional connection you have with money, I'll be inviting you to take a good hard look at how you really feel about money. Your feelings are a clue to your unconscious beliefs. Once you uncover your unconscious blocks to wealth, you will be in a much better position to remove them.

Understanding that everything around us is energy, vibrating at different levels, and that like attracts like, you now need to find out how you are currently vibrating on the subject of money. Once you understand your vibration (thoughts and beliefs) about money, you are then in a position to change the frequency.

In all the exercises that follow it is crucial to be open and honest with yourself. Take the first answer that comes to you and write it down immediately, no matter how strange it may sound to you. It may bring up some emotion for you. You may feel sadness or anger. You may even shed some tears. That's OK. It takes courage to confront your beliefs around money, so be kind and gentle with yourself. It is only by facing up to your old beliefs about money that you can start to transform them into more empowering beliefs. It is then that you can become a Money Magnet.

Exercise: Touching the Money

This exercise is one that I have used with great success at the "How to Become a Money Magnet!" workshops. It originally came from some of the people on the workshop and it makes an excellent opener to the tricky subject of money. It can also take you straight to your core beliefs about money.

I am going to ask you four questions.

Before I do so, please can you make sure that you're in a comfortable seated position, where you cannot be easily distracted. Take out a banknote and hold it in your non-writing hand. Have a pen and a blank sheet of paper at the ready.

Take three deep breaths and allow your whole body to relax. Clear your mind of any distractions from the day and be still. When you are totally clear and ready, ask yourself the first question and then immediately write down anything that comes into your mind, no matter how ridiculous it may sound.

At your own pace, progress through the four questions. Make sure that you "clear" your mind and relax fully in between each question. This is a contemplative exercise and should not be rushed.

Are you ready?

Question 1: Money, how do I really feel about you?

Question 2: Money, how do I treat you?

Question 3: Money, how can I have more of you?

Question 4: What else would you like to tell me, money?

OK, how was that for you? Did you uncover any surprises or interesting insights about your feelings toward money? If not, it doesn't matter. Just doing this exercise in itself opens you to the possibility of attracting more money.

If you're not sure whether you've done the exercise correctly, don't worry. There are no correct answers. Just allow your answers to come from your heart rather than your head. This is not an intellectual exercise. Whatever you have written is a reflection of your thoughts around money. It is your truth. However, to give you some examples, here are my answers from the very first time I did this exercise many years ago.

Question 1: Money, How do I really feel about you?

"Money is disposable, purple, glittering silver, precious, loved, plentiful, not to be defaced or abused, handled by many."

Question 2: Money, how do I treat you?

"With love and respect, with joy, with gratitude, with pride; carelessly at times; sometimes I'm too boastful about you or too trusting."

Question 3: Money, how can I have more of you?

"Smile more, go out more, love more, give more, share more. I need to believe in you; rejoice, for life is plentiful; plan to have more of you; accept you; greet you like a good friend."

Question 4: What else would you like to tell me, money?

"Don't be afraid of having more; you are good enough. Think big. Give big. Accept big rewards. I am good, I am a thank-you, I am holy, I am love. Love is energy and you have lots of it."

Remember, the above responses are just examples, not instructions. You will find your own words and inspiration. You will uncover your own truths about money.

With this initial exercise you are starting to tap into what you really think about money. Of course, the tricky bit, as you have already learned, is that at least 80 percent of your thoughts are subconscious.

Remember, while you may consciously wish to be rich, your subconscious may hold what it considers to be good evidence that being rich doesn't actually make you happy. In such an example, your subconscious is keeping you from being unhappy. Your subconscious thoughts could be "protecting" you from feeling rich!

Tomorrow you will uncover more about your current thought patterns on money, so that you can change them as quickly as possible.

The money is already there. The only thing preventing you from being rich is *you*.

DAY 4

How Do You Feel About Money? (Part 2)

Yesterday you gained a clearer idea of your true thoughts about money from the exercise we did. Today we're going to build on that by exploring your beliefs on money further.

Let's get started straight away with another exercise. It is crucial that you don't cheat by including any preparation beforehand or by looking at the others' answers that follow. Doing so would weaken the power of any insights gained. For the following exercise you will need a blank piece of paper cut or torn into smaller strips.

Exercise: Money Beliefs

Jot down quickly any thoughts that come to mind about money, ideally each one on a separate piece of paper. Use the questions below as a prompt.

What were you told as a child about money?

What did money mean to you as you were growing up?

What's your favorite saying about money?

What comes to mind when you read about wealthy people?

Who is your role model for attracting money? Describe the person.

Now divide the pieces of paper into two piles, one representing positive statements and the other representing negative statements.

If you have more negative than positive statements, it offers an explanation as to why you are attracting less money than you wish. You are literally vibrating at a frequency that will only attract a limited amount of money.

Please complete this exercise before reading further. (You can simply read the book, but you increase your chance of success by doing the exercises in it!)

If you have more positive statements than negative and you are still unhappy with the amount of money in your life, we simply need to raise the bar—we'll look at how to do this later in the book.

Don't beat yourself up if you've carried on reading without completing the exercise. Give yourself a break. Take some time out now to quickly jot down how you feel about money. Respond to the questions in the previous exercise. It will only take you a few minutes and it could pave the way to a more abundant life.

If you keep rushing through life, you risk missing the most important bits. You miss hearing your inner voice. You'll mistake external circumstances and other people's opinions for the truth. Many of our beliefs about money stem from our families, our national and religious heritages, our friends and our colleagues. Take some time to listen in to what beliefs you have taken on board. Isn't it time to take a moment to listen to yourself?

Congratulations if you completed the exercise before reading on! Your commitment to becoming a Money Magnet will lead to faster results.

Below you will find some of the responses from people who've attended the "How to Become a Money Magnet!" workshop. It will be interesting to compare your responses and look out for any common themes. Very often our beliefs about money come from what we were told as children. Can you remember who educated you first about money? What did they say was the most important thing about money? Was it important to enjoy it or to save it? Were you expected to work hard for your money or were you taught that you'd always be looked after?

Negative Statements about Money

- "Money doesn't grow on trees."

- "It is easier for a camel to pass through the eye of a needle than for a rich man to enter the kingdom of heaven."

- "Filthy rich."

- "It's impolite to discuss money."

- "There's never enough money."

- "We can't afford it."

- "I never have enough."

- "Only the rich get rich and the poor get poorer."

- "Born with a silver spoon."

- "You don't get something for nothing!"

- "You have to work hard to be rich."

- "Money is the root of all evil."

- "I hate taxes."

- "True wealth has nothing to do with money."

Positive Statements about Money

- "I am a Money Magnet!"

- "I've always been lucky."

- "I'm good at what I do."

- "I deserve to be rich."

- "Money buys you time."

These beliefs are accepted at a young age as being the truth. Now is the time to flush out these learned beliefs. Then you can go on to decide for yourself whether these are empowering beliefs or not. You can then consciously select only the positive beliefs about money that will transform you into a Money Magnet.

Money for Money's Sake

Listening to many of the negative statements about money over the years, I've found that the general consensus is that "money for money's sake" is not a good thing.

The Bible's proclamation about the rich man and the camel through the eye of a needle suggests that the pursuit of money for money's sake can distract us from what is really important, and I agree. But you can still be a Money Magnet. It's just all about the "vibe" that you're giving out!

Have you ever noticed how some people just seem to behave in a confident way, whereas others have their heads bowed? Which type of behavior do you think is most likely to attract financial opportunities and lucky breaks?

If you feel you don't deserve to be rich, you never will be, even if you win the lottery. Look at the many people who have won millions on the lottery, only to let it slip through their fingers in no time at all, often resulting in being worse off than previously.

Winning the Lottery

Winning the lottery is what most people think of when they think of attracting money. They are focused on the money, and often on the huge unlikelihood of actually winning! It's not surprising then that they fall at the first hurdle. However, you can use the idea of winning the lottery as a way to discover what you really want from life. By imagining what it would be like to *feel* like a lottery winner, you have a way to discover why you *want* to be a Money Magnet and why you *deserve* to be a Money Magnet. Wanting money just to have money is not healthy and will rarely work.

Exercise: Make Your Own Lottery List

If you won $15 million on the lottery, what would you spend it on? Taking your pen and some paper, compile a list of all the things you would really like to do if you scooped that jackpot. Enjoy this exercise. It's fun to play make-believe!

It might help you to ask yourself the following questions:

Would you live your life differently?

How would money empower you?

How would you being rich benefit the world?

Would your money disappear as quickly as it arrived?

HINT: If you no longer needed to get out of bed in the morning, your life would be the poorer for it (life is about living, not sleeping!)

Holding a vision of what you would do with money is a far more efficient way of attracting money than focusing on the money itself.

The money is already there. The only thing preventing you from being rich is *you*.

DAY 5

The Value of Money

Our attitudes to money are underpinned by the value we give it, both consciously and unconsciously. This is the topic we shall explore today.

How you feel about money will have an effect on how much of it you attract. The more grateful you are for the money you have, the more money you are likely to attract.

To get an idea of the true value you place on money, answer the following questions:

- How much do you think you value your money?

- Do you work hard for your money or does it come to you easily?

- Are you cautious in your spending or do you like to splash out once in a while?

- Do you know how much money is in your wallet right now?

- What are your feelings about the cash in your wallet?

- Is it enough?

- Do you feel wealthy?

When you receive money in exchange for something you value, like your job, your home, or your car, you are likely to value the money received. If your job, your home, or your car is no longer loved or appreciated, this may lower your expected value of it, and in turn the money you receive for it. The amount you value your money can be directly proportionate to how much you value what you've provided in exchange for the money.

It is easier to believe that you can have more money in your life if you feel that you deserve to receive more and if you feel that you have more to offer the world. The amount of money you have is a reflection of the amount of value you have for yourself.

Value Yourself More

When you value and love yourself, you are wealthy and you will attract wealth.

Now, you may be saying to yourself, "I do value myself, so why am I not attracting more money into my life?" Before we go on to look at your precise beliefs about money, let's take a moment to look at where you could be valuing yourself more.

Are you valuing yourself in terms of your health, the work you do, and in the relationships that you have? Are you choosing activities that you love to do? Are you allowing others to love you? How are you demonstrating respect for yourself on a daily basis?

Write down five ways in which you are *not* valuing yourself. What could you do differently?

Write down five ways in which you *are* currently valuing yourself. How could you do more to value yourself?

You are now ready to look at any specific limiting beliefs that you are harboring toward money itself. By shedding some light on these barriers to your wealth, you'll be in a position to "kick them over" and get back on your pathway to riches.

Exercise: Why Are You Not Attracting More Money into Your Life?

Take a pen and write down all the benefits of having *little* or *less* money you can think of. (In a moment you'll read some of the responses collected from people on the "How to Become a Money Magnet!" workshops, but try not to look before you have completed the exercise yourself.)

Now have a look at some of the answers I received at my workshops.

Some Benefits of Having Little Money

- Fewer costs.

- Fewer/no taxes.

- Fewer responsibilities.

- Nicer person.

- Mix with nicer people.

- More spiritual: "I am always provided for."

- Pay less for items; become an expert bargain-hunter.

- Receive more gifts.

- Loved for who I am.

- Fewer bad habits as can't afford them!

If you've struggled with the above exercise, try the next one. In fact, try it anyway! I now want you to think about and write down the problems you associate with having lots of money. (Again, try not to look at the responses below that came from my workshops before you have completed the exercise yourself.)

Some Problems with Having Lots of Money

- People only love you for your money.

- Fewer real friends, shallow friendships.

- Distances you from your "roots."

- Lose touch with reality.

- No sense of purpose.

- Added responsibilities.

- Need to employ accountants, etc.

- More tax.

- Too much choice: which car, which home, etc.

- In the public arena.

- Less time.

- Less privacy.

These very powerful exercises will help you to find what has been in the way of you becoming a Money Magnet.

The Power of Belief

By now you should be gaining some real insights into how you feel about money and, as a result, why you have as little or as much money as you do in the bank.

Your beliefs are so powerful. They direct your unconscious thought patterns, which in turn create your reality.

Remaining a prisoner to your beliefs limits your power to become a Money Magnet. Taking responsibility for what is in your life, and the beliefs that created it, is the route to freedom and abundance.

Look at some of the beliefs that you wrote down earlier. What would your life be like without them? Is there a general theme to your limiting beliefs? Maybe a thought that you don't love yourself enough to earn more, or that you're just not worth a higher income? Is there one belief holding you back most from attracting money? What is it? Write it down, as you may need to refer back to it later.

In running the "How to Become a Money Magnet!" workshops with hundreds of students, we found that there was one common belief statement for most of us. This does not preclude other beliefs, but it does suggest that most of us carry a similar burden. This belief is: "I am not good enough."

Does that resonate with you? Is there part of you nodding in agreement, even if another part of you is protesting? Is your head responding in one way and your heart another? What does it mean to you to think, "I am not good enough"? Does it mean that you are not worthy? Or that you don't love yourself enough? Does it mean you're not worth the going rate, or that your colleagues deserve to be paid more than you? Does it mean that you don't value yourself or what you do any more? Does it mean that, inside of you, you know that you're no longer giving your best effort? Does it mean that you are resigned to your fate—that you have given up? Does it mean that you will never be good enough so there's no longer any point in trying? Maybe somebody told you a long time ago that you were not good enough and you took that comment on board as though it were the truth.

The lower your self-value, the lower your attraction for money.

Grab a piece of paper and start a written conversation between you and your emotions. It is time to get to know the real you and to flush out all the "clutter" of your limiting beliefs. Your emotions act as signposts along the way. Trust them and question them to find your answers. Only *you* have access to your truth. Nobody can do this for you. It is time to trust yourself.

Recognize that a low sense of self-worth is lowering your "money vibration." In holding on to your limiting beliefs, you are resisting the opportunity to have a rich and successful life. Letting go of any belief that you are not good enough is the gateway to the life of your dreams.

The money is already there. The only thing preventing you from being rich is *you*.

DAY 6

How Much Money?

Today you're going to take a more detailed look at your finances and consider how much money you'd like to have.

How much money do you actually have, right now? Do you know? Do you have at least a vague idea?

If you don't know where the starting line is, you won't be in the best position to run the race. Some would disagree with me here. After all, you want to attract more money into your life, so what does it matter where you start from?

We don't include balance sheets on the "How to Become a Money Magnet!" workshops, but in my own experience, taking time to "face up" to your money is all part of conquering any limiting beliefs that you have around money and its influence on your life.

Exercise: "My Money Bank" List

Take your pen and paper and write out the list below. Draw a line down the page so that there are two columns for two sets of answers. Fill it the first column to the best of your ability, without checking your accounts or statements.

- Current account(s).

- Savings account(s).

- Shared account(s).

- Mortgage account (equity).

- Internet account.

- Premium Bonds.

- Shares property.

- Investments business.

- Investments.

- Other investments.

- Piggy bank.

- Monies owed to me.

Now complete the list again in the second column, this time accurately, by referring to any relevant papers or accounts. For some of you, this may involve clearing out drawers-full of old papers.

Clear space to do it now. Need an incentive? The last time I checked my accounts, I found a large investment in Premium Bonds that I'd completely forgotten about. Sounds ridiculous? Have a go yourself and see what you can find.

What's your total worth? Are you feeling wealthier yet? You may find that you are a millionaire already and you didn't even know it!

Exercise: Create Your Own "I Attract Money" List

If you have been focusing on the lack of money in your life, this is the moment where you shift your focus.

Again, you may need to double-check your papers as well as your memory. In addition to any regular dependable income you receive each month, maybe from different sources, I'd like you to remember any times in the last six months when you have attracted money from somewhere else. This could have been a gift, a tip, a bonus, or an extra opportunity for which you received money, e.g. babysitting, selling goods on eBay, commission on a one-off brokered deal or some after-hours training for a colleague.

Many of my clients regularly find money literally lying in the street! Have you "accidentally" found any cash in the last few months?

Now take a pen and paper, jot down the following lists, and fill them in.

Regular Income

- Salary (full-time).

- Salary (part-time).

- Real-estate rental income.

- Income from shares.

Additional Income

- Gifts or inheritance.

- State benefits.

- The sale of private items.

- One-off projects.

- Temporary jobs.

- "Discovered" cash, e.g. on the street or in forgotten accounts.

- Money back on goods purchased.

- Free money with a loyalty card (I *love* getting money off my shopping at supermarkets!).

Needless to say, the above lists are not for accounts or tax purposes. They are for your eyes only, as we assess the current strength of your Money Magnet.

As your mind expands to the many different ways in which you can attract money into your life, you will start to notice even more and, bit by bit, the power of your magnet will grow.

Real Money and "Pretend" Money

Some proponents of the Law of Attraction emphasize that it's good to spend money whenever you wish to. They present the case that "If you act like a wealthy person, you'll be vibrating as one and will therefore attract more wealth into your life." To some extent that may be true.

However, if you are spending money that you know, on some level, you don't have, this will not work. Remember, it is not so much the conscious thought—for example, "I feel wealthy indulging in this treat"—as the unconscious thought—"I shouldn't really be spending this money right now"—that creates your financial reality.

In today's credit-crazed society, it can be tricky simply spending your own money and not someone else's. If you've ever owned a credit card, you'll know the experience of "paying" for something without feeling like you're really parting with any cash. It's easy to up your spending on the spur of the moment to something more expensive.

This is what I refer to as "pretend" money. It is not the same as making a conscious decision to borrow money for a specific purpose. It is living beyond your means, and it does not come into the remit of being a Money Magnet.

If you use credit cards, take the time now to check how much debt you have. Yes, "debt" is a nasty word, acting like a drain on your magnetic energies. It's like filling up a bucket with money, only to discover that you're leaking (those will be the interest payments) out of the bottom!

Act on your debt now in order to plug that hole!

Somewhere in your subconscious, debt will hold you back from being a true money magnet, so take the following actions, where appropriate:

- Pay off all outstanding credit card balances each month.

- Always pay off more than the minimum payment each month.

- Pay off the balances with the highest interest rate first.

- Look at transferring high-rate balances to a low-rate or zero-percent card (check the transfer fee and the rate for any incumbent balance on the low-rate card).

- Keep a close check on your financial status each month.

- If you are struggling, get some help: negotiate with the credit card companies.

- Look to spend less and attract more real money.

- Start making friends with money again and spend a week using only cash.

The money is already there. The only thing preventing you from being rich is *you*.

DAY 7

Money Magnets and Spending

To vibrate as a Money Magnet, it helps if we adopt some of the behaviors of wealthy people. Most wealthy people I know count the pennies and let the pounds look after themselves. Today our topic is Money Magnets and spending.

Did you hear about Duncan Bannatyne, the self-made millionaire who is one of the dragons from the TV series *Dragons' Den*? Despite his incredible wealth and the success of his companies, Duncan once asked his staff not to purchase any paperclips—he reckoned they could save money by collecting paperclips from the morning's post instead!

How do the wealthy approach spending? The answer is: creatively.

Exercise: Spending Creatively

Before we can get creative, we need to know how much we are playing with. Do you know how much money you actually spend? If you are not sure, carry out these initial steps first and start to spend time with your new friend, money:

- Carry a notepad with you for a week to monitor your spending.

- Transfer all your spending totals into a monthly expenditure chart (an Excel spreadsheet is a big help with this).

- Gather similar items into groups, such as: regular bills, entertainment, miscellaneous.

- Select a number of key items from the list, as it's now time to get creative and to think like a Money Magnet.

When I looked at my various expenditure items, I soon realized where I was overspending in a few areas (see opposite).

Expenditure item	Small action	OK action	Significant action
Gas	Check prices on web	Share lifts to work	Buy a more efficient car
Lunch	Take packed lunch to work	Eat less!	Change jobs for one with a cheap or free canteen
Books	Use the library	Share books with friends	Donate books to charity shops (and maybe pick up one or two as well!)

For each of your expenditures, come up with a creative way of having the item but spending less, thereby leaving you more money in your bank account. Go on, be a little daring and venture outside your comfort zone—after all, it's only an exercise! If you prefer, you could play a variation of this exercise with friends, where each one of you has to come up with a fresh idea for each item. You could even award bonus points for those with the most innovative or unusual ideas. The trick is to get those creative juices flowing!

Here are some ideas I had for cutting my expenditure:

- **Supermarket food shop:** I buy mostly perishable organic fruit and vegetables. The trouble was that I couldn't resist a bargain! I would buy "two for the price of one" or a whole bag of oranges instead of the couple that would actually get eaten during the week. Of course, much of it perished before the end of the week. It was like throwing money down the drain!

- **Books:** I was a sucker for a good book. Bookshops were my equivalent of candy stores. I gradually became friends with my local library. I then started to let go of the books clogging up my home by lending them out to friends. If they came back, I reasoned that they were meant to stay with me.

- **Seminars:** Have you heard the expression "seminar junkie"? Well, I'd like to think that I wasn't that bad. However, when I realized that I was going to workshops on how to write a book rather than actually writing a book, I knew something had to stop! I still go to workshops and retreats, as it's my favorite way to learn something and to meet like-minded people. However, now I set myself goals to complete first!

OK, so we've looked at the amount of money you are currently attracting, and at some of your beliefs about money. Remember, the two are linked. Later we'll look at transforming your old money beliefs so that you can start to attract more money.

Before we do that, though, let me ask you: Are you clear about how much money you really want?

"Yes, of course I am!" I hear you exclaim. If so, write down the exact figure on some paper, and include the date when you will have this money, like this:

By .... (date), I expect to have $............. in my personal bank account.

- How did you reach that figure?

- Did you compare yourself with someone else?

- Did you simply pluck the figure out of "thin air"?

- If you are truly expecting a certain amount, don't you think it may require a little more thought?

- What will that amount of money enable you to do with your life?

- How will it serve both you and others?

- How will it improve you as a person?

Vision

Many people talk of attracting $15 million on the lottery. What would you do differently with $15 million?

A part of you knows that if you won the lottery tomorrow, you could relax and take life easy. The problem is that you weren't born on this earth to remain stagnant. We all yearn to grow and to become *all* that we can be. Sometimes the desire for money and security will push us to achieve much more than we initially think we can achieve. But then, what do we do once we've achieved it?

If we fully understand *why* we wish to achieve a certain amount of money and we feel that it is a deserving reason, we are more likely to attract the money we desire.

It's important to maintain a vision at all times. By keeping a vision of where we are going we will keep moving forward and growing. Be clear about what you want from the beginning and this book will help you get there.

I am constantly amazed by the number of people who tell me that they want to have more money. Yet when I ask them, "How much money?", they have no answer. Sometimes they quickly grab a figure out of the air, maybe the amount announced on TV the night before or a number that reflects a friend's ambition and is no reflection of what they really want.

If you want something in your life, you need to be clear about what it is, whether it's money, winning a race, or publishing a book in 30 different languages. That means investing time in your dreams and getting your vision clear. Remember, it's you and nobody else who creates your life. Maybe it's time to start mastering your thoughts on the subject of "Me and My Life."

The money is already there. The only thing preventing you from being rich is *you*.

DAY 8

Changing Your Habits

Over the past seven days you've looked at how your thoughts create your reality. You've explored the beliefs that you currently hold about money and about being wealthy. You took time to look at your current financial circumstances. By doing so, you gained an insight into how your thoughts have created your circumstances, and not the other way round. Now it's time to change your mind about money, so today we're examining how to change your habits.

If you wish to change the results in your life, you need to change the thoughts that have created those results. By changing your thoughts about money, you can transform yourself into a Money Magnet!

Are you ready to change your mind about money? Are you ready to let go of limiting beliefs and well-worn phrases? Are you prepared to behave differently around money?

It takes courage to change a life pattern. We live in a society of the quick, easy fix. We want to be transformed simply by reading a book. Your brain chooses the option with the least resistance. Your natural tendency is to stay in the "comfort zone" that you've created for yourself. Thinking the same thoughts perpetuates a cycle in our lives.

So, to become a Money Magnet you need to adopt a different approach. To change your financial circumstances dramatically, you need to change your thoughts and your beliefs about money dramatically. You need to clear out the clutter of old, limiting thoughts to create space for new possibilities.

The Power of Ceremony

One of the most powerful ingredients of my workshops is the use of ceremony to release old beliefs and to set an intention for a new era of abundance. Sometimes this is all that's needed and the results can start to manifest within 24 hours.

Ceremony works on both our conscious and unconscious thoughts, which is why it can be so effective in changing a habit.

It can feel a little silly performing a ceremony, but that's the whole point. It can be an uncomfortable process and, as such, it pushes us beyond our normal comfort zone—it literally shifts our energetic vibration!

Performing a ceremony is like lifting a signpost up to the universe to announce the start of a new pattern. It can be very powerful.

What Makes Up a Ceremony?

The main ingredients of an effective ceremony are intention and ritual.

Think of some of the ceremonies inherent in our culture and how powerful they can be in changing our lives. The ceremony of marriage can be so powerful that the connection remains very strong even in the case of divorce. For this reason, it can be a good idea to perform a type of ceremony to recognize divorce.

Many of our culture's traditional ceremonies are dying out, and without ceremony we risk losing our focus on what is important.

This book is about money. I wonder if you already have any rituals with your money? For example, do you always pay all your bills on a particular day each month? Do you use a certain desk? When you go to see your bank manager, do you wear a well-chosen outfit and take the car rather than walk?

Do note that if you have no rituals around money, you may not be treating it with enough respect. Resolve today to build in some rituals to the way you handle your money. For example, schedule a regular time to do your bills each month or to check your expenditure and earnings sheets, and do these things in a way that makes you happy.

Enhancing Rituals with Intentions

We all use some ritual in our lives, from cleaning our teeth to washing the dishes. The trick is to enhance the power of a ritual by combining it with powerful thoughts.

For example, when paying your bills, take enough time to get comfortable at your favorite chair and desk. Maybe use your very special "lucky" pen. Then take a few moments and a few deep breaths, and reflect on your ability to pay these bills. Think of how fortunate you are to have attracted what money you have to pay the bills. Consider how lucky you are to have a roof over your head and food on your plate. Dwell a short while on all that you have for which you are grateful. Gratitude breeds more gratitude. You are celebrating your wealth every time you pay for something.

Money is simply energy. It is meant to flow from one person to another. Paying your bills keeps the flow going and creates space for new riches to come into your life. Enjoy paying your bills and enhance that enjoyment with the use of ceremony.

Let me share with you some guidelines and examples that I have used over the years, to help you get a feel for the key elements involved.

The "How to Become a Money Magnet!" Ceremony

Inevitably, a ceremony is considerably enhanced when it is witnessed by several people. If we make a statement to ourselves, it will have less power than if we share our statement with another, and even more power if we share our wishes with our family, our friends, or any other supportive group.

Each "How to Become a Money Magnet!" workshop ceremony is created by the people in the room at the time, each person contributing an idea or an action for the whole group.

Typical contributions include solemnly lighting a candle for each person, providing a shoulder massage for each participant, reading out a poem or creating a flower arrangement. We adapt the ceremony to the season, so that in summer we often walk over to some nearby woods and use the river in our ceremony.

At the core of the ceremony is the opportunity for each person to declare solemnly to the group that he or she is now letting go of old, inhibiting money beliefs such as "I'm not good enough to receive." The person will then symbolically dispose of these old beliefs. Ways of doing this have included ceremoniously placing a written copy of an old belief into a fire or into a river stream to be washed away. Feel free to be creative with how you wish to do this.

Ceremony Guidelines

- Set aside plenty of time.

- Plan ahead so that you have everything you need to hand.

- Incorporate elements that are special to you, whether these are objects, poetry or specific movements.

- Have a clear intention about whether to clear or to attract something, or both, one after the other.

- Where possible, announce out loud your intention, ideally to witnesses.

- Be fully present, whether you're performing the ceremony or present as a witness.

- Incorporate elements that are outside your normal behavior or environment.

You can create your own ceremonies at home or in the office—wherever feels right for you. So come on, take the plunge, and celebrate the start of your new era of abundance!

The money is already there. The only thing preventing you from being rich is *you*.

DAY 9

Breaking the Pattern

Today we are looking at ways in which to break the pattern of our thinking to make room for attracting more money.

As well as running "How to Become a Money Magnet!" workshops and life coaching, I am also a Feng Shui consultant, and in this context I often use "space clearing" to help shift old beliefs and stagnant situations. Space clearing is a way of shifting the energy in a room or home or even an office. It is traditionally done using Native American sage.

Lighting the sage, in the form of a "smudge stick", you waft the smoky aroma through the space, all the time maintaining your intention to clear all negative or limiting energy.

Doing Something Out of the Ordinary

Maybe space clearing just isn't your thing; it all sounds just a little too wacky for you.

If this is the case, then instead I recommend that you find a way to do something *new*, something different, something that's a change from your normal routine or way of doing things. When you do something outside of your normal patterns it serves as a wake-up call to your energetic pattern and can open up a chance for change.

Anything that takes you out of your comfort zone is good, whether it's walking on hot coals or actually paying your bills on time!

Of course, it's not comfortable to step outside our comfort zone. Instead, many of us settle into our nests of "affordability." We persuade ourselves that we're OK as we are, that we can get by, even if we haven't got as much money as we'd like.

Sooner or later, however, the level of buried dissatisfaction will reach breaking point and we'll feel we simply have to do something about our situation. It's a bit like the alcoholic who will ignore their drinking problem for as long as they can, but sooner or later the "nest" becomes intolerable and they are finally ready to risk jumping out. In jumping out, in doing something totally different to all previous behavior, they just may learn to fly.

And so it is with money.

"Poor Me!" Becomes "Lucky Me!"

As I have already mentioned, attracting money is easy. If we haven't enough money in our lives, it is evidence that we are not thinking "wealthy" thoughts.

Fortunately I realized this early on in my career and, using what I knew, I was able to achieve considerable financial success.

However, some years ago I made a mistake and invested in a house with someone who was inherently unreliable. He stripped the house of everything and then vanished. I was left with a house worth substantially less than I had invested, and I descended into the depths of "poor me."

I stopped working for three months and invested all my cash savings to put the property back together again. As I painted the walls myself, I reinforced the "martyr" thinking of "poor me." The more I thought "poor me," the more money seemed to pour out of my bank account into this house. When I realized that with no money left I was going to have to move into the house, I knew that I needed to create a dramatic shift in the energy!

The day that the carpets were due to be laid, I arrived at the house very early in the morning. My intention was to let go of the "poor me" and to welcome in a new era of abundance. I needed a ceremony that was radical for me and totally different to anything I had previously done. I needed a drastic shift in my energy and in my belief systems!

Taking one of the leftover tins of white paint, I started painting the wooden staircase steps where the carpet was to be laid. On the first step went the word "welcome." On the second step the word "joy," and on the third step "peace." I carried on, painting a different word on each step, finishing with "abundance," which literally seemed to "dance" into the bathroom.

Then I started on the wooden floorboards of the landing with "thank you." Having spent months berating the lack of help with the house, I now painted the floor with the name of each person who had helped me with the home, even starting with the name of my unreliable partner, without whom I wouldn't have had the home in the first place. I continued to paint love and inspiration symbols in one bedroom, and money signs in the second bedroom. When I was finished painting, I danced around the house singing out loud the words I had written. And as I sang, I felt a shift in how I felt about the house and about my circumstances.

The results were immediate—and I think I may have shifted my beliefs about men as well as about money! An ex-boyfriend appeared that day and took me to lunch. He was unusually amorous! Then a gas man arrived to do a job on the house and asked me out. Then the carpet men arrived and offered me the most expensive underlay for free.

I soon realized that far from being in a nightmare situation, thanks to my original decision I was now lucky enough to be living rent-free and mortgage-free. The effort and money that I'd used meant that I was not only living mortgage-free but I had a brand-new bathroom and kitchen, and a wonderful new layout to my home. Wasn't I the lucky one?

Using the power of ceremony, I had shifted from "poor me" to "lucky me." If you don't like the results that you are manifesting in your life, be honest about your thought patterns and do something radical to shift them.

Here are some ideas for doing something new:

- If you've always been employed, why not consider becoming self-employed?

- If you're self-employed, why not collaborate and think bigger solutions?

- If you've always wanted to be a published author, why not start writing?

- If you've always wanted to have the home of your dreams, why not start saving?

- If you've never had enough money, why not invest in changing your beliefs about money?

- If you're full of great ideas but never seem to get started on them, use a coach to help you with the process of turning each idea into reality.

What is it that you're not doing, and that you know you could do, to improve your financial situation, right now?

Next time your heart jumps for joy, honor its desire.

The money is already there. The only thing preventing you from being rich is *you*.

DAY 10

The Power of Intention

Today's topic is the power of intention.

If you haven't yet done something different, take a moment and write down the one thing that you will do now to start to change your approach to money.

Too many people exclaim, "Oh, I want to have more money!" without ever getting specific enough. Without any clear intention, such a comment is but a wish, at best. At worst, the statement might as well be, "If only I had more money!" This is the same as saying, "I'll never have more than I have now." While the conscious words may state a request or even an intention for money, the unconscious intention is to remain with the status quo.

To shift this state of paralysis, we need to get specific, and we need to include a time frame.

Similarly, by setting a time limit and being clear on when you will have this money, it will become easier to manifest it.

Exercise:
Stretching the Possibilities

How much would you like in your bank account? Now multiply that figure by 10 and imagine receiving that amount of money. How does it feel? Does it feel uncomfortable? (It can be too big a leap for most people.) Now think back to your original sum and double it.

Odds are that the new higher figure doesn't feel too uncomfortable now, even though only minutes earlier half that figure was the maximum that you could imagine receiving.

Once the mind is stretched, it cannot go back to its original state.

Whatever it is that you want, however much money you would like to have in your bank accounts, sooner or later the next step is to *set an intention*.

In other words, you reach a moment of decision. You get clear on exactly what you want and you decide to attract it, usually by a certain date. In setting an intention, you commit to it happening. You shift from a position of "maybe it will happen" to "I know that it can happen." Having a clear expectation of what you truly desire is a key step in the process of becoming a Money Magnet.

Using Clear Intentions to Achieve Sales Targets

Whenever we have a clear intention, we make it easier for the "universe" to assist us. I learned this technique from my earlier years as a sales manager. Rewarded with exciting incentives, there was always enough motivation to achieve the set target of sales per month.

The trick is to anticipate it, even when the evidence may be saying otherwise!

Often with a monthly sales target of over $1.5 million revenue, my sales team would achieve it in the very last few minutes of the month! They were exciting times, and as long as we stayed 100 percent focused on achieving the target, we achieved it.

Similarly, when we were promised bonuses for exceptional sales performance, I would often spend my bonus money before I actually received it. Quite simply, I expected to receive it, so I acted as though I had actually been guaranteed it. The intention was clearly set for me to receive that exact amount. I behaved as though it was already "in the bag"— and I always did receive it. Always.

What are you expecting to receive financially over the next month? Would you like to set a new intention?

We often feel limited by outside constraints: "Oh, my firm would never pay me money if I decided to leave my job." "Nobody's ever earned that much in this job." "I'm just not that lucky."

Watch out for comments like these and discard them the moment you become aware of them. Start believing in miracles. Start small if need be, but start to push the boundaries of what you think may be possible. Always set an intention for what you really want, not for what you think you'll be able to achieve. There's a big difference between the two.

Let me share an example with you. At work I was responsible for more than 80 percent of the company's sales, and though I always achieved my targets and was well paid, I'd become bored with the job and, in my heart, I knew that I was ready to move on.

The problem was saying "no" to a comfortable salary and all the perks that came with it. I decided that I'd feel a lot happier leaving work if I could leave with an extra bonus.

Leaving for a two-week vacation, I discreetly cleared my office of all my personal items, acting as if I wouldn't be returning after the vacation. During the vacation itself, I became clearer and clearer that I wouldn't be returning to work, and the figure of $45,000 became ingrained in my mind. I had no idea *how* I would actually leave the job, as I still couldn't actually see myself resigning. But I kept the intention of leaving work and the figure of $45,000 in my mind.

On the night of my return, my boss called to ask if I could meet him at a café before coming to the office next day. I remember feeling delighted and telling my sister that I would be back within the hour. After sharing my future plans with my boss, he actually agreed with me that my dream of doing even more traveling was what was right for me just then. I said, "I can't afford to leave the job, though," to which he replied, "How much would you need?" I was taken aback, but answered, "Well, about $45,000." To my astonishment, he answered, "Well, OK, for the person who has been responsible for over 80 percent of the company's business, I'd say that's fair enough!" Within the hour I'd left my job with a promise of over $45,000 coming my way. I only ever went back to the office for my leaving party!

Remember: Set an intention for what you really want, NOT for what you think you'll be able to achieve. It doesn't matter whether what you want has been achieved beforehand. All that matters is that you are clear on what you want. It's good to have a timescale and a good reason why you want what you want. Then it is simply a question of taking one step after another as each one presents itself.

The money is already there. The only thing preventing you from being rich is *you*.

DAY 11

Expecting More Money

We saw yesterday that the key to attracting more money is to *expect* it. But you may be wondering how you can suddenly start expecting more money if the external evidence suggests otherwise.

So, let's start today by recapping that you can expect more money because so far you have:

- Read and digested the information to this point in the book.

- Become responsible for your finances by checking your accounts.

- Performed a ceremony to mark the start of a new way of thinking about money.

- Done something different to attract more money.

- Let go of "how" it will happen.

- Had a clear intention to attract a certain amount.

- Behaved "as if" you expect more money.

Is it a coincidence that we find the money just when we need it? What about all those times when we don't find money? If you set a clear enough intention and you truly expect the result, then you will always find the money. The trick, of course, is to manage your thoughts. You need thoughts of anticipation rather than hope. You need thoughts of expectation rather than desire.

Take the example of my friend Molly, a training consultant, who wished to be employed by one of the major banks. Molly stated her intention by writing herself a check from the bank in question for $300,000. She dated the check and pinned it on her notice board.

Two years later she realized that she had, in fact, attracted a total sum of $300,000 earnings from this particular bank over the previous two years. Looking at her notice board, Molly noticed that the check was dated for that year.

Case Study: Intention Releases Available Funds

Joanna decided to redecorate her main bedroom. Her intention was clear and she went ahead and started to clear the room in anticipation. The fact that Joanna didn't have any spare money to pay for the redecoration did not deter her from her objective. She didn't allow her circumstances to influence her thoughts. She expected to accomplish the task.

Imagine Joanna's satisfaction when, on clearing the bedroom, she came across $600 cash on top of the wardrobe. It was the perfect amount to pay for her bedroom's redecoration!

Your subconscious mind sees what it sees. What it sees influences the subconscious thought, which then endeavors to create the reality of what it sees. In the above example Molly's subconscious mind saw the check and so expected it to be real. Her thoughts then set about creating that reality.

What are you looking at every day? Does it reflect the reality that you desire? How can you improve things?

As a Feng Shui consultant, I advise people on how their surroundings can support their desires. I am often called in when life is not running smoothly, and I'll find the clues on the walls in the home.

Case Study: Art of Influence

Hannah and her husband were marketing consultants who had moved from Leeds, in the north of England, to London 10 months earlier. Unfortunately, they hadn't been able to sell their beautiful five-bedroomed home in Leeds. This meant they had the considerable expense of running two homes, and money seemed to be trickling away from Hannah and her husband.

When I visited the home in Leeds, I discovered a collection of old pictures lacking any color and featuring images of people weighed down by the burden of extreme poverty. They were very depressing.

Needless to say, I recommended their immediate removal, and the fortunes of Hannah and her husband improved. The house was sold and they were able to enjoy their new life in London.

Vision Boards

Why not collect images of how your life would look with more money? Collect images of experiences that make you smile and that you would like to attract into your life. Arrange them attractively on a board or in a picture frame so that you can glance at them every day. Then you can simply leave it to your subconscious to work out a way to attract those specific things, giving you a "nudge" along the way when you need to do something different.

In the film *The Secret*, we see James Ray moving into a spectacular new house. Among the boxes being unpacked, his son discovers James's old vision boards. On one of the vision boards, made some years earlier, is a picture of the exact house that has just become their new home.

Create yourself a vision board and get yourself into a position where you expect riches!

Case Study: Vision Boards Do Work

Mitch in Canada was an agent for aspiring authors. He kept a vision board in his office, where he collected pictures of everything that he wished to experience in his life. On it were pictures of the Bahamas, the Cayman Islands and Jamaica. He also had the name of a specific cruise liner.

One day he received a call from his client and friend, Peggy, inviting him to join her on a cruise. Have you guessed?

The cruise ship was visiting the exact destinations featured on Mitch's vision board! It even turned out to be the exact cruise company that was featured on Mitch's vision board.

Of course, one of the best ways to influence your thoughts is through the language you use. This brings us neatly to the next chapter, and how you can change your language to attract more money.

The money is already there. The only thing preventing you from being rich is *you*.

DAY 12

Becoming Rich

Listening to the language you use, whether on paper, in speech, or in the way you think, can help you to become a Money Magnet. Your mind, body and spirit are intrinsically linked. In choosing your words carefully, you can choose to feel more positive. Your positive feelings will then act as a magnet, attracting more reasons to feel positive. Today we will explore how you can use your words and feelings to become more attractive to money.

Riches are coming your way. Be as you would be if you knew that you were due to come into some money. No doubt you would feel happier with life and less stressed. Imagine for a moment that you wake up tomorrow morning to open a letter in the post, and the letter announces that you are receiving an unexpected win of $15 million.

Now *pause* to really feel what this feels like. Are you smiling? Or maybe laughing hysterically? Has your body relaxed? Can you feel joy in your bones? How does it feel to be rich? Get into the feeling. It feels good, doesn't it? See how long you can continue feeling "as if" you are now rich. A friend calls you. Do you tell her your news or do you simply smile inwardly? Are you different in the way you respond to her? How are you different?

People who know that they have enough money will behave differently to those who worry about where the next penny is coming from. They will think differently, behave differently and speak differently. They may hold themselves more confidently. They may have more time to listen to others. They may have more confidence in taking occasional risks. They may trust their judgment more easily than those with less money do.

I'd like you to list some ways in which a wealthy person behaves differently to a person with less money.

On Day 2 you discovered that everything is made up of energy, and that the difference between one thing and another is a difference of vibration. We are like magnets attracting similar vibrations. "Like attracts like," and "What goes round, comes round," are common expressions in our language. Your thoughts, feelings, language, and actions are all at a certain vibration level. In order to become a Money Magnet, you need to think, feel, speak, and act as though you already are a Money Magnet. It's simple.

"No, not that simple," I hear you exclaim. "If it were that simple, wouldn't we all be rich by now?"

The answer is: yes. Yes it is simple, and yes we can all be rich. In fact, we were born to be rich. In this chapter we'll look at what you can do to start feeling rich straight away.

Before you look at changing your vibration, let's take a very brief moment to look at how you *don't* wish to be.

Take a few moments to answer the following questions:

- How would you feel, speak and act if you felt that you didn't have enough money?

- Did you try to get hold of this book at a discount or even for free by borrowing it from the library or a friend?

- Do you always take the cheapest quote or do you shop around for the best service?

- Are you ever resentful or jealous of another's success?

- How often do you complain about life being unfair?

- Are you surrounded by friends who boast about the bargains they find?

- Have you ever been accused of being a cheapskate?

Do you recognize any of your own behavior in the above list? Be courageously honest. It's time to acknowledge how you are attracting a life with less fortune, simply in the way that you are behaving (or vibrating, to be exact).

Let me share an example. My friend Stevie and I decided to go on Bob Proctor's Caribbean cruise. The cheapest cabins were $1,200 for the week. However, neither of us wanted to stay in a cabin with no sea view or balcony. So we set an intention to pay only $1,200 for an upgraded cabin and, because we expected it, that's what we received (see Days 10 and 11).

We were naturally thrilled with our mastery of the situation… that is, until we started talking to other guests on the ship. We then realized that some of them had paid even less money for their cabins! Now we weren't feeling quite so happy, or masterful, or rich. Now we were starting to let feelings of resentment creep in.

The cruise included talks from a number of motivational speakers, and one day we heard the speaker Paul Martinelli share his secrets for success. One secret in particular stood out: "Accept the Going Price."

His principle was that when you want something, you value it, and you are happy to pay for it: simple. That's how a wealthy person would behave. And in understanding this truth, our energies shifted back to a higher vibration.

Within the next hour I overheard a woman sharing how she had been upgraded to VIP status as a result of paying more for her cabin than others. It didn't take me long to act on this and get Stevie and myself upgraded to VIP status, which included a gift worth $2,000 and private morning sessions with Bob Proctor!

As soon as we shifted our approach to the situation, we then attracted the better situation. Easy!

Let's look at your scenario. What is it in your life that you wish to improve? What are you thinking about your current financial circumstances? How can you change the way you are currently thinking about the situation?

Often when we dwell on a negative statement, it leads to another, and another. It snowballs until things are really bad.

If we share our bad news with a friend, we double the negative energy that we're devoting to it (unless you choose that friend very carefully!).

Don't focus all your energies on why things are not good. Instead, look for the positives. Then you will no longer be a match for the negative vibration, and either the job will change or the other person will change.

Exercise: Accentuate the Positive

Write down at least three negative statements about your current situation. Then cross them out and replace them with a positive version of each statement.

For example: "I can't afford to buy that book I really wanted" is crossed out to become "I'm so lucky to live in a country with free access to library books whenever I wish."

The crossing-out of the negative statement is important. It signals to your subconscious that the negative statement is no longer valid.

Changing the pattern of your thoughts takes practice. You have to be totally committed to manifesting a better life for yourself. And I've found that it helps to have a coach or a good friend who will keep you on track.

My mother knew that a couple of years earlier I'd felt that I'd made a poor investment decision and my bad habit was to complain about it. So she cut out some text from a magazine and pasted it onto the back of one of my late father's business cards. These were the words:

> *It's pointless to have regrets. If you took a decision for a good reason at the time, that was the best you could do so there's no point regretting it.*

It stopped me in my tracks and it helped me to stop my negative thinking. We all need a friend or a coach to point us in the right direction every now and again.

The money is already there. The only thing preventing you from being rich is *you*.

DAY 13

Improving Your Reality
with Your Mind

Today we will look at how important it is to "be" wealthy, so that wealth comes to you.

Start the day, while still in bed, with some happy, grateful thoughts. Focus on one of your goals and imagine for a few moments that you have already achieved that goal. Feel what it feels like in every cell of your body. Enjoy the happy sensation as much as you can.

Greet yourself in the mirror with a big smile. Check your thoughts while in the shower and getting dressed. If a negative thought sneaks in, acknowledge it and let it go. Get curious about how you can find positives where before you only found negatives. This can be particularly effective when your negative thoughts are about another person. As you think positively about him or her, that person is far more likely to meet your positive expectations.

I was having negative thoughts about how little my partner did around the house. These thoughts were definitely sapping my energy levels. Once I realized what I was doing, the next morning I found a way to think more positively about my partner and his contribution to the house. That very evening, with no word from me, he returned from work and immediately started cleaning the oven and then the shower! It was indeed a miracle, and evidence yet again as to the power of our thoughts.

Why not try it at home with your partner or friend?

You can apply the same principles in a work situation. Simply by changing your thoughts about the situation at work, you can improve it.

Affirmations

A relatively easy way to help you change how you think and feel about your situation is to change what you *say* about your situation. This is where the use of affirmations can be helpful. An affirmation is a simple positive statement that is repeated on a regular basis until the mind adopts it as a new belief. Some people like to keep copies of their favorite affirmations in places where they can see them regularly, for example inside a kitchen cupboard or written in secret code on the steering wheel of their car.

Examples of affirmations for becoming a Money Magnet include the following:

- If you want to change your situation, start changing your thoughts about it *now*!

- I am (now) a Money Magnet!

- I'm always finding money.

- I attract money wherever I go.

- I am happy, healthy, and wealthy.

- I love my life.

- I have all that I need and more.

- I deserve lots of money.

- I love money and all that it allows me to do.

- I respect money and money respects me.

- I make money easily.

- I value what I do.

- I offer enormous value.

- I am happy to receive my full worth.

Choose the affirmations that feel most comfortable for you and remember to say them as often as you can.

Self-Worth

The link between your feelings of self-worth and being a Money Magnet is so essential that it's a good idea to look at it again. You may be holding back your natural flow of abundance through a lack of self-worth.

Looking back, I've enjoyed periods in my life when I've attracted huge amounts of money and success… and then I've done something to sabotage it. The up-and-down cycle of my wealth was an indicator of how worthy I felt as an individual. Once I understood this, it was much easier to do something about it, using many of the techniques in this book.

Find an affirmation that starts to build your self-confidence. My personal favorite is "I'm OK just as I am." It just seems to roll off my tongue without trying too hard, and I can noticeably feel my body relaxing when I say or think it.

Exercise: Create Your Own Affirmations

Some people respond best to their own affirmations. So now I'd like you to create your own affirmations, and have fun putting together words that, when used often enough, can literally transform your life!

Follow these guidelines:

- Keep it personal, using "I" where it's natural to do so.

- Keep it simple.

- Keep it natural and something that you would find easy to say often.

- Give it a rhyme or rhythm.

- Keep it positive ("I'm giving up being broke" is negative).

- Keep it in your natural language.

- Keep it credible.

If you are saying "I am wealthy" as an affirmation and yet, every time you say it, you have a little voice in your head exclaiming

"Yeah, right! Have you seen your bank balance lately?" then it won't be a very effective affirmation! In fact it could even have the opposite effect to the one desired. An alternative affirmation might be, "I'm ready to receive more wealth into my life." As things start to improve, you may then adjust your affirmation to "I'm starting to attract more money." This may become "I am a Money Magnet!" which may then lead to "I am wealthy!"

Participants who've completed the "How to Become a Money Magnet!" course are able to say, "I am a Money Magnet!" The fact that they have been on the course is evidence in itself that this is now a credible statement. In the same way, once you have read and inwardly digested this book and completed the exercises, you too will be able to affirm, "I am a Money Magnet!"

What affirmation would make the biggest difference to your life?

Write it down and start using it *now*.

The Be-Do-Have Principle

Are you waiting to have money in the bank before you do the thing you've always wanted to do and be as happy as you can be? Are you miserable in your job but waiting until things are better financially before you leave? Have you always wanted to write a book but are waiting until you have enough time? Are you waiting until you're rich to be happy?

If you can relate to the above comments and you are waiting to have something before you can be happy, you've got it the wrong way round! Maybe that's why you haven't progressed as much as you'd like. Maybe that's why you feel "true happiness" is avoiding you.

The principle of Be-Do-Have is that you have to *be* the person you want to be first, in order to then *do* as that person would do, in order to then *have* all that you want to have.

If you start to behave as a lucky person, for example, you will start to attract luck wherever you go. You become a magnet for good fortune. You may then have the confidence to take decisions that you may not have made before you considered yourself lucky, and you will attract things into your life that you've always wanted.

Rather than waiting until you are wealthier, you can decide to be happy and wealthy right now. Today, you can be happy if you really want to be happy. Look around for something that is good about you or your life. Look to nature and find something beautiful that will make you smile. Think of the last time you were laughing and feel that joy inside again. By choosing to be happy now, you will attract things to do and to have that make you happy. Remember, it's all in the vibes that you're giving out. Be a magnet for happiness and you will be a magnet for money.

If you wish to be a Money Magnet, start emitting the vibes of someone who has money. Be generous from the heart and you will naturally attract more money. Be grateful for all the amazing abundance that you already have in your life: your health, your sight, your loved ones. Behave like someone who is confident in their ability to make money and you will attract the opportunities to make it. Bemoan your situation and the opportunities will do a U-turn at the end of your street.

Be rich in your dealings with others and you will become rich in what you have in your life. It's the Be-Do-Have Principle! Resolve to apply it in your life now.

The money is already there. The only thing preventing you from being rich is *you*.

DAY 14

Freeing Up Space

In Feng Shui we look at the energy of a home and how it flows from room to room. When there is clutter, it slows down the energy. Have you noticed how someone with a lot of clutter in the home is often tired and never seems to have enough money? Today our topic is how to free up space to attract more energy.

Money is energy. If you wish to have more money, you need to create space for new energy. That space may be in your home or your office. It may be in your schedule. It may be in your thoughts. Let's look at them all.

People often ask me, as a Feng Shui consultant, "What is the one thing that I can do to get more money?"

Without question, I advise them: "Go home and start clearing your clutter. Make way for some new energy to enter your life." For many people, clearing their clutter is the turning point toward becoming a Money Magnet.

My book *Creating Space for Miracles* covers this subject in much more depth, but let's start with the basics: What is clutter? What is your clutter? When are you going to clear it?

What Is Clutter?

Clutter is the stuff in our homes and in our heads that gets in the way of us living the life we desire. The Feng Shui Academy definition of clutter is: anything that is not loved, not useful or not kept in an orderly manner.

If it helps, keep this definition posted up somewhere in your home until you have cleared all your clutter.

You know, better than anyone else, where the clutter is in your home. What is your worst clutter? Is it the collection of unread magazines, the unworn clothes in the wardrobe or the stack of unwanted presents? Where does everything get hidden when you don't know what to do with it? Is it the garage, the loft or the spare bedroom that needs clearing? If your bedroom is cluttered, make it a priority area to be cleared. It will be giving your mind all the wrong messages as you fall asleep and make you more likely to wake up feeling exhausted.

Maybe your home is free of physical clutter. To the external eye, it is clutter-free. How about your handbag or briefcase? What is the state of your car? How about your email inbox?

When Are You Going to Clear It?

Well done for facing up to the clutter in your home. The next step, of course, is to set about clearing it. When are you planning to be free of clutter? Where and when will you start? What will you need in order to clear the clutter? Bin bags, a skip, a helping hand, the "drop off" times of your local charity shops, and so on. Make a list of what you'll need, mark the date in your calendar and commit to it.

Make way for wealth—commit to clearing your clutter now!

Exercise: The Clutter-Clearing Contract

Taking a pen and some paper, write down: "I commit to clear my clutter now." Now list all the clutter you need to clear. Next, identify the steps you need to take in order to clear it. And finally, sign and date the following statement:

"I commit to clearing my identified clutter on [insert date]."

Then sign and date your "clutter-clearing contract" and if possible, get someone else to sign it as a witness.

By making a formal "contract" with yourself, you send a signal to your subconscious that you are serious about this action, and you are therefore more likely to see it through.

Living in a seriously cluttered space will sap you of energy. It becomes a "chicken and egg" scenario, where you no longer have the energy to clear the clutter while the clutter continues to drain you of any energy that you do have.

On top of feeling constantly "under the weather", you may find your finances are suffering, too. In fact it is a shame that clutter-clearing services aren't funded by the government, as they could have a huge positive impact on our communities.

Once you have made the decision to clear your clutter, you are more likely to find a way to get it cleared. Remember, clearing your clutter is a huge step forward to becoming a Money Magnet.

The good news is that almost as soon as you clear a space, the laws of nature dictate that it will be filled. If you combine your clutter-clearing with an intention to attract wealth, the "void" is more likely to be filled with the energy of money.

Clutter in Your Business

The same rules apply: if you have cluttered up your business with too much office clutter, too many products and too many people, it needs clearing. We all have to shed the unnecessary clutter in our lives to make way for progress and to create wealth.

The money is already there. The only thing preventing you from being rich is *you*.

DAY 15

Clearing Away
Mental Clutter

It's not just clutter in your physical environment that's keeping you from attracting more money. It's also clutter in the way you live your life and how you think. Today, we're going to look at how to clear our mental clutter.

Let's start by seeing where we can clear some space for more money in certain areas in your life that may have become cluttered and which may now be consuming too much of your energy. Take a look at the list below and jot down any that apply to you.

- Time-consuming friendships that you no longer value.

- Unnecessarily long telephone calls.

- TV—you know which programs we're talking about here!

- Everyday tasks that you take on when you could choose not to.

- Never-ending "to do" lists.

- Magazines and books that need to be read—or do they?

- Emails that need to be answered—or not, as the case may be.

- Subscription email newsletters that you haven't the time to read.

- Social or work commitments that no longer lift your spirits.

- Concerns about never being "good enough."

- Out-of-date grudges, guilt, blame, or any negative emotion.

- Gossip.

- Thinking about all the clutter that needs sorting!

Now, for each one that you have written down, write out underneath at least one alternative way of being. For example, if you feel guilty about something, decide to forgive yourself. If you are wasting energy blaming somebody, look instead for the positives in that person. If you don't wish to spend your time cleaning, think of alternative ways that the cleaning can get done. Practice thinking outside the box to come up with ways to maximize the time you have available to be a Money Magnet.

If you ticked 'TV', make a note of how many hours you spend watching television, then select what you now choose to watch. Make it a conscious choice. Many programs today are littered with bad news, poverty, and violence. Are stories like this really going to help you to become a Money Magnet?

Unless you have already gained mastery over your thoughts in a way that can resist such messages, I suggest that you seriously limit your intake of television. Instead, choose to do something that lifts your spirits, whether that be reading a book or taking up dancing.

Focus Clears Mental Clutter

The easiest way to clear your mental clutter is to go back to the basics of "What do I really want?" and "What makes me feel happy?"

When you focus on what is important to you, you can clear the clutter that is getting in your way. If your "to do" list is full of items that bore you or that seem more like daily chores, then you will find yourself going round in circles, never making any progress toward your goals.

Your focus needs to link directly to your goals. For example, if your goal is to attract $150,000 into your bank account by the end of the year, your daily priorities will include at least one item that supports that goal, whether it be studying for a new qualification or telephoning a new prospect.

If you're not sure what you really want, don't worry! We'll be taking a closer look at that in the next chapter. In the meantime you may wish to look at your daily activities and make a list of what you *don't* want to do any more. By writing it down, you will be one step closer to clearing this type of clutter from your life—and anything that doesn't make you happy can be termed clutter.

Exercise: The Daily Time Audit

Note down in a diary for a week how you spend your time each day. At the end of the week, categorize the different activities under column headings such as: Fitness, Work, Household, Finance, Friends, Intimacy... You can choose your own headings.

Are your activities evenly balanced across all columns? Is any activity consuming too much of your time? Would it be beneficial to reduce the time spent on this activity? Where would you reallocate the extra time you now have?

Resolve to make the necessary changes now.

Clear "To Do" Lists

Nearly everyone I know uses "to do" lists. Unfortunately, they often only succeed in making you feel exhausted. If you are going to bed with a picture in your mind of that never-ending list of things to do, you won't have the energy to do what you really want to do.

Instead, write down all the things that need doing as they come into your head during the day. Let's clear some space in your head for more important things, such as the inspiration that may lead you to attracting more money!

At the end of each day, find your list and decide on the top three things that need doing the next day. By choosing only three items, you will become better and better at prioritizing and you will start clearing the clutter that's been holding you back. Remember, your daily priorities are those items that will move you forward or that will attract money, if that is one of your goals.

Keep Your Focus

When your focus is to attract more money, you have a yardstick by which to judge where you choose to place your effort. For example, given the choice between spending time writing this book and having a telephone chat with a friend, the book becomes my priority. I will schedule the chat with a friend as a reward once this chapter is completed. Similarly, if you earn more money per hour than you would pay a cleaner, you may choose to hire a cleaner.

In the next couple of days, I will expand on this subject as I elaborate on why it's important to follow your passion, to prioritize what is important to you, and why taking action is the fastest way to cut through any clutter and become a Money Magnet!

The money is already there. The only thing preventing you from being rich is *you*.

DAY 16

Following Your Passion

Today our subject is following your passion. This is the master route to becoming a Money Magnet. Anything less than this and the money manifested is likely to be temporary. Congratulations on reaching this part of the book and this point in your life.

As we have seen, you can attract money by setting an intention, by performing a ceremony, and by doing something different to your normal routine. You can start expecting to be rich and you can change your language and behaviors accordingly, but until you clear the clutter that's keeping you from your heart's desires, any money you attract will be just that: money. And as money is energy, it can disappear as soon it arrives, unless you uncover your own stream of abundance.

We have determined that money is received in exchange for value. Finding your gifts to the world and the best way to add real value is the secret to feeling truly fulfilled and wealthy in every sense. When you lift yourself toward your highest potential, you can become a Money Magnet. Funnily enough, the money arrives almost as an afterthought, as you become driven less by money and more by passion.

Money is worthless in itself. Someone stranded on a remote island for the rest of her life would be silly to wish to be a Money Magnet in those circumstances. Money flows to us when we are in our flow. We receive rewards for living at our highest possible potential, whatever that may be. A desire for money can distract us from our true passion, but it can also inspire us to lift our game in life and be all that we were born to be.

How do you find your passion? How do you find your flow? The answer to finding your flow is to follow what makes you happy.

"Well," I hear you ask. "If it's that easy, why aren't we all richer?"

The answer is that most of us think we are doing what we want to do, but we are actually just playing it safe. It is a basic human need to want to be safe. We learned at a young age how to keep our main provider happy. Mummy was happy when we did what she wanted us to do. With our basic needs at stake, we learned how to please others from very early on and, in time, those other voices became so many that they drowned out the sound of our own personal and authentic voice. It's not surprising in this context that many people lose sight of their own identity.

Fortunately, this way of living is difficult and exhausting to sustain and so, sooner or later, many of us will experience what I refer to as a mid-life wake-up call. This is the moment when you catch a glimpse of your true self and from which there is no turning back.

The Mid-Life Wake-Up Call

How many people do you know who have ended up in a career because someone else, somewhere along the line, recommended it as the ideal route for them to take? It may have been a parent, a guardian, a peer, or a teacher. They took the recommended option, only to "wake up" mid-life and realize that it wasn't what they would have chosen for themselves. They are the lucky ones. Some people persevere in a job and live a life full of regret. Remember, you can't take the money with you.

Recently I was coaching Rachael, a woman in her sixties who had just "woken up." She remembered going to a public phone box at the age of 15 to make a call to a local rock band looking for a lead singer. She never made that call. When we explored her true desires, being a professional singer was still top of her list. The only difference was that now she was learning to trust herself and to honor her heart's desires. She knew that it might not always be plain sailing up ahead, but turning her back on herself again was no longer an option for her. Rachael is finally focusing on what truly makes her happy.

It's amazing how committed you will be to a task when you are fuelled by passion!

- Do you know what truly makes you happy?

- When was the last time you felt joy or passion?

- What makes you leap out of bed in the morning?

- What are the events you are always on time for? (Lateness, no matter what the excuse, is a sign of your reluctance to be there.)

- What is it that you think you want to do?

- Is your heart really in what you do or want to do?

Finding out what really makes us happy can be challenging. One of the ways to get clearer on what you want is to start by looking at what you *don't* want.

Exercise: Finding Out What You Want (by Looking at What You *Don't* Want!)

Make a list of all the things currently in your life that you don't want: a boss you don't like, large household bills, a relationship that is going nowhere. It is important that you now rewrite your list, but this time reframe each item into a positive statement of what you do want: a great boss, enough money to do whatever you'd like to do, a committed, loving relationship. As you write out each new positive statement, cross out the item that you didn't want.

Forget the Money and Focus on Your Passion

So, you're reading a book entitled *21 Days to Become a Money Magnet* and I'm telling you to forget the money? Yes, that's right! By all means, set an intention of how much money you wish to manifest and take responsibility for how much money you currently have. Follow all the steps in this book so far. And then be prepared to let go of your financial dream and to trust that when you follow your passion, it will happen.

Miracle Club

Two years ago, I received the inspiration for Miracle Club. It was to be a worldwide network of people supporting each other to achieve their full potential. Combining the principle of the Law of Attraction with the practice of group coaching sessions, it would create a haven of positive thought. It was a brilliant vision and I told everyone I knew about Miracle Club.

I registered the company and then I was advised to do a business plan to work out how it was going to earn me some money. Nothing happened. I never seemed to have the time or the confidence to get round to doing this business plan. I was distracted by so many other things and by what everyone else around me was doing.

Miracles happen when you follow your passion!

One day I finally realized that I really was the happiest I could ever be when I was inspiring others to believe in themselves and in their dreams. Whenever one of my students told me another story of his or her success, my heart seemed to explode with joy. So instead of asking, "How can I earn money from this?" I asked myself a different question: "How can I make a real difference using my skill and passion?"

I realized that the people who needed Miracle Club the most were those with the least money to pay for it. I wanted to reach the people who had given up on their dreams, who had lost their jobs and who had no money. Once I was clear on what I really wanted, I set an intention to attract funding for Miracle Club. Within a week, I found a sponsor to fund places on Miracle Club... and Miracle Club was officially born!

Now is the time to find your passion and to let it explode into a gift for the rest of humanity. You were not born to play small or to live a boring life. You have a natural desire to be happy and to grow into your full potential. Now is the time to wake up and start getting excited about every single day of your life!

The money is already there. The only thing preventing you from being rich is *you*.

DAY 17

Finding Your Heart's Desire

When we are happy, our energy shifts to a higher vibration. We start to attract more things that make us happy. So, it makes sense for you to find out what will make you the happiest — and then start from there. Today we're going to explore how you can find your heart's desire

Don't think "How?", think "Wow!"

Instead of asking yourself, "How can I earn money from this?", ask, "How can I make a real difference using my skill and passion?"

Finding out what you really want can be quite challenging if you haven't done it for a while. Let's start with the following exercise, which is based on one described by Jack Canfield in his book *The Power of Focus*.

Exercise: Finding Your Immediate Heart's Desire

Write out a list of 101 things that you want to be, do or have. Start with 40 things. Then add another 30, and then a final 30. Add a last item just to tip you over the 100 mark.

The first 40 items may be relatively easy to think up, but the secret to success in this exercise is to reach at least 101 items.

Only once you have your full list, select all the short-term items that you would like within the next year. Rewrite them onto a separate list on the far left-hand side of a blank piece of paper. Now in true "knock-out tournament" style, take two items at a time and, as fast as you can, select the one that you want more. It is important to complete this exercise at great speed. If possible, compete with a friend to see who finishes first.

Your first answer is likely to be your heart's desire. If you take longer, it allows time for your brain to get engaged and the exercise won't work. Continue the process to the bottom of the list and then start again with the chosen options, and again until eventually you reach the top eight, four, two and eventually your top number one priority for right now.

Phew! Now you can relax! The rest will be so easy…

I remember the first time I did this exercise. My list was full of impressive ideals, and yet my number one priority was to lose weight! I was hugely disappointed. "How shallow," I thought. Then I realized that if I were to take the necessary steps to slim down, it would mean that I would be showing more respect for myself. And yes, self-respect was a good number one for my list!

The second time I did this exercise I discovered a new desire: I wanted to have the chance to present a regular slot on radio where I could inspire others to think more positively and to take responsibility for their reality.

One of the main benefits of the 101 exercise is that it invites you to think outside of your normal comfort zone. The first 40, even 60, are likely to be familiar to you. When you complete the exercise to the full 101, or more, you may uncover heart's desires that you were previously unaware of.

Enjoy the freedom of exploration as you create your list. Follow your heart, not your head.

Find Your Heart's Desire and the Money Will Come

Katie came to me for Feng Shui coaching. She wanted to run her own interior design business—at least, that's what she told me when we first met. When we ran through her

101 list, her heart's desire turned out to be to own a camper van! Her face lit up with joy at the very mention of it.

I asked Katie, "What do you need to do next in order to own your own camper van?"

"Oh," she said. "I need to get a job." (I told you this was simple!)

"And do you have any particular job in mind?" I asked.

"Oh, yes," Katie said. "I know of the perfect job that I can do. I just need to make one phone call and the job is mine."

It was incredible. Katie already had the means to her end. She'd just been looking in the wrong direction! She hadn't paid full attention to her true heart's desire.

I enquired whether the job was something that she really wanted to do.

"Oh, yes," she said again. "It's with my favorite charity. I already donate money to them and it will be a real joy to spend my time getting other people to contribute to a cause that I believe in. I think I'll be really good at it!"

Once you get clear on what you really want, everything starts to fall into place. Attracting what you need, including money, becomes easy.

The Challenge of Following Your Heart's Desire

First of all, you need to be clear of clutter so that you can feel your heart's desire and know your true passion. We are often distracted by the expectations of others, or by "just getting on with it."

You have to be prepared to accept that what was your passion at one time might now have shifted to something else, and that's completely OK.

You need to honor your heart's desire by having the self-belief and focus to act upon it. Sometimes it's far less scary to fail at something when your heart just isn't in it than when it's a desire that goes to the very core of your being.

In the next chapter we'll look at bringing together all the pieces of the puzzle in what I call the FAB process.

The money is already there. The only thing preventing you from being rich is *you*.

DAY 18

The FAB Principle

If you want to be a Money Magnet, you want to get into the How of what makes you feel happy and fulfilled. Or, in my language, whatever gives you an incredible buzz! So today we're going to concentrate on the FAB principle. F-A-B stands for Focus, Action, and Belief. In brief, you want to *focus* on what is important to you, you want to take *action,* and you want to *believe* in yourself and your goals. It is simple, really.

Case Study: Richard Branson Acts on His Passion and Belief

At a very young age and to encourage the development of his character, Richard was dropped off a mile from home and left to find his own way back. What an inspiring lesson in encouraging self-belief. Unlike most of us, who learned how to survive by keeping others happy, in that instance Richard learned that he could actually rely on his own judgment, independent of others.

Throughout an incredibly successful career, Richard has consistently followed his heart's desires, often in complete contrast to the wishes of his advisors and family. He demonstrates belief in himself and in his visions. He stays focused on the vision and achieves it by literally taking one step at a time. He is driven more by passion than money, and yet Richard Branson is a perfect example of a Money Magnet.

For more about Richard Branson's inspiring life, take a look at his autobiography, *Losing My Virginity* (Virgin Books, 2007).

Once you've identified your heart's desire, you need to take some action. This may seem obvious, but I'm regularly amazed by students who have read books on the Law of Attraction and who believe that they can become wealthy purely by the use of visualization.

Visualization *is* a very powerful tool. Just ask any athlete. When you expect to be rich and you feel what it would feel like to be rich, you will then start to attract opportunities to be rich. Effectively, you will have transformed yourself into an energetic Money Magnet.

Now, to make it real, you need to *act* on the opportunities presented to you. An athlete may visualize winning the Olympics, but unless she takes enough action to ensure she gets a place on the team, she can't win Olympic Gold no matter how much she has visualized standing on the podium.

Interestingly, the action you take is not always directly linked to the result. That doesn't matter. All you need to do is start taking steps toward your goal and the opportunities will present themselves.

What Are the First Action Steps You Could Take?

- Have you done an audit of your finances?

- Have you cleared your clutter?

- Did you ask for that promotion?

- Have you prepared your CV for that job?

- Have you made the phone call that needs making?

- Have you started that book that needs writing?

- Have you written your business plan?

- Can you get up an hour earlier just to start doing some of these things?

Our minds get cluttered up with irrelevant detail. We can go full days, even weeks, without making any progress toward our goals. Once you have found what's important to you, whether it's losing weight, starting a business, writing a book or saving 10 percent of your earnings each month, keep a tight focus on it. Every morning, wake up and remind yourself what is most important to you. I often think about this in terms of having three key priorities. For example, my top three at the moment are:

- Finish this book.

- Weigh 10 stone.

- Achieve $150,000.

So, a typical day at the moment will start with me writing. However, I build in an opportunity for exercise sometime in the day, usually with a friend. By the way, I would only ever choose to do exercise that makes me happy. My favorites at the moment are going for bike rides, brisk walking into town and belly dancing. The only other thing that I will allow to interrupt my writing will be anything that is related to maximizing my income. Again, I am only referring to items that make me happy. These could be delivering a public talk, coaching a client, or running a Miracle Club class.

Life is about balance. Some people may argue that one should focus on only one thing at a time until it's finished. Yes, I agree, as long as you allow some breaks in the process. Interrupting my writing to see a friend for a bike ride or to coach a client often provides me with just the inspiration that I need to continue.

When you start every day focused on specific goals, you have more chance of success and you create more free time for recreation. It's easier to say no to activities that are not aligned to your goals, and to say yes to fun activities, when you know that you've done your best toward your goal that day.

Over the last few days we've looked at how important it is to uncover your passion and your gifts in order to become a true Money Magnet. We've looked at how to find your heart's immediate desire, and some of you may have found that it isn't actually "money" after all. Taking what you found to be the most important focus for you at this moment in time, commit to taking the steps needed to allow it to happen.

Exercise: Focused Action

State your top three immediate desires. Put a timescale on each one, such as "I'm going to have $75,000 in my bank account in September," or "I'm going to be presenting on TV before the end of this year."

Take a moment to *feel* what it's like to have achieved this goal.

Now, for each item, write down one thing that you're going to do today to attract this possibility. And do it.

Before you retire to bed this evening, take your three priorities again and write down another three immediate actions, one for each vision, for the following day. Only change the focus once your heart is happy that it has been achieved.

Taking action is the quickest way to clear the clutter that's stopping you from being all you can be. Taking action is less about "making it happen" and more about responding to life's opportunities.

"So what about all the people who are following their passion and yet can't find two pennies to rub together?" I hear you ask; "What about the struggling artist or writer, the massage therapist, the chef who dreams of owning his own restaurant? Where are they going wrong?"

They are stopping just short of their potential. They will go as far as the cliff edge but they may be afraid to jump off it. Their lack of money is the clue that there is more for them to do. In order for us all to reach our full potential, we have to be prepared to abandon our comfort zone.

By pushing yourself to do something challenging that may make you feel uncomfortable and even a little scared, you will burst through your comfort zone. As your comfort zone grows, so does your capacity for increased wealth. Don't settle for being comfortable when you have so much more to give to the world. Seize the challenge of being the best you can be and go for it!

The good news is that if you have found your passion and you are good at it, the FAB principle will ensure that you become a Money Magnet. Keep focused on your dream, start taking some positive action toward it and believe in yourself and your goals. One final tip: if you still have a nagging suspicion that you're just not good enough to aim so high, pretend for the moment that you are good enough, and do it anyway. Get used to bursting through your redundant comfort zone!

The money is already there. The only thing preventing you from being rich is *you*.

DAY 19

Value Yourself and You Will Attract Value

As we have already learned, money is about an exchange of value, so our topic today is how a strong sense of self-worth is key to becoming a Money Magnet.

Do you truly think that you're worth more than you're currently receiving? Your thoughts are what have created your current reality. The good news is that if you have found your passion and you're good at it, you have the potential to become a Money Magnet.

Make an intention to become a Money Magnet. Mark the shift with a ceremony of some sort or by doing something radically different to your normal behavior to mark the moment. Start to expect more money to come to you and change the way you talk about your situation. Use affirmations and visualizations to support your transition. And most of all, act now to clear your clutter! It could be the only thing that's left standing in the way of your success.

Case Study: You Are the Only Obstacle to Your Success

Sharon became one of my clients after hearing me give a talk entitled "I'm Following My Passion, Now Where's the Money?" Hearing me, she suddenly realized why she was struggling financially with her business.

"It's me," she said to her friends. "I'm the only thing standing in the way of my success. It's me!" Her friends looked on blankly. They didn't understand. "Isn't it the economic climate or the lack of business funding that is at fault?"

Following her moment of clarity, Sharon booked in for three months of coaching. She cleared the pattern of "poor me" that had plagued her since she was small. Sharon took responsibility for her thoughts and for her life to date. In doing so, she cleared the way to becoming a Money Magnet.

Almost immediately Sharon started attracting lucrative opportunities for her business.

The more you love yourself, the more you will have to give to others. The more you value yourself, the more value you will have to offer others.

• Do you value your gifts?

• Do you appreciate all your strengths?

• What is it that you can offer to others that will make a difference?

• What is it that makes you really happy? Do it.

Decide now to start valuing yourself more. You are a precious commodity and worthy of being looked after. What do you need to perform at your highest? What drives you? Take some time to really get to know yourself.

Make a list of your strengths and skills. Ask a friend, if you need to.

Include all your qualifications and achievements to date, and anything good that anyone has ever said about you.

How Good Are You at Receiving?

Can you remember how you responded the last time someone paid you a compliment? I've overheard so many people reject the positive vibration being sent their way.

For example, "I love the dress you're wearing."

"This old thing? I bought it reduced in the sale two summers ago."

Or "Congratulations on your new job. What an achievement!"

"Oh, it was nothing really… just in the right place at the right time, I guess."

Next time the person paying the compliment might just not bother. After all, the "knock-back" of the compliment is effectively down-valuing their point of view. How silly of them to have thought it was a lovely dress when it was only a two-year-old sale bargain? How stupid was it to imply that you have done well when the job was always "in the bag"?

When you receive a compliment yourself, practice receiving it graciously with a simple "Thank you." Practice receiving and allow the "gift" to settle. A quick retort to a compliment is a bit like spending all your wages as soon as you get them. Allow some time for appreciation.

When the money comes knocking on your door, are you ready to receive it as graciously as you would a compliment? When the inspiration for a new business idea comes into your head, are you ready to accept it or are you thinking "That's a great idea —for someone else"?

You are offered plenty of opportunities to attract more money into your life. You just need to turn around, open your eyes, stretch out your arms and say, "Thank you!"

Now might be a good time to start practicing the art of receiving.

Exercise: Get Ready to Receive

- Are you really ready to receive lots of money?

- Are you ready to give your gifts to the world and to receive your true worth?

- Do you have a sneaky idea of exactly what you need to do next in your life in order to attract more money? If so, write it down *now*.

It may also be worth asking yourself, "How often do I accept or request help with my life, my home, my business?" Many of us try to do it all ourselves. To become a Money Magnet, you need to let go a little so that you can start to receive more openly.

Letting Go

Letting go of wanting to become a Money Magnet is all part of the process. You can let go when you know that you already are a Money Magnet!

You attract whatever you think about. You now think that you are worth so much more than when you first picked up this book. You know your true value and you value yourself. You have an inner knowing that is about to manifest in your outer world. Keep that faith and let go of being a "wannabe!"

The money is already there. The only thing preventing you from being rich is *you*.

DAY 20

Staying on Track

So, you've been reading this book and you've taken in all the information, done all the exercises, and changed your way of thinking. You're well on the way to becoming a Money Magnet. But how do you maintain momentum and stay on track? That is our topic for today.

It sounds easy to stay in touch with what we really want, but how many times have you fallen by the wayside? Perhaps you've gone along with the crowd, just for the sake of convenience? Maybe you'd love to leave your job but it feels scary to be without the regular pay packet, so you've held off taking action? In order to stay connected to abundance, you have to start honoring your own desires. Listen to your truth, listen to what you really want, and then take just one step toward achieving it right now. Look for the one action that feels the most uncomfortable and scary. When you take that one step toward your dreams, you will feel a huge sense of relief. You will know that you are on track. Avoid the scary step outside of your comfort zone and you risk going round in the same circle forever.

The trap is when you look at what you currently have rather than what you wish to have. You stay in the same job in order to have money. If you are miserable in the job, your thoughts will not be the kind to attract money—you are likely to attract redundancy or ill-health. Sickness is often a sign from your body that you are ignoring yourself.

Case Study: Ill-Health Is Your Body Shouting at You

Debbie arrived at the class out of breath and overweight. She told us how her job was making her ill. She was working too many hours, because "it won't get done if I don't do it." She told us how she'd love to leave her job but they couldn't afford to have one less salary in the family. In fact she didn't dare tell her husband that she didn't want to do the job any more.

Can you see now where Debbie was going wrong? Debbie had been ignoring her heart's desires for so long that her body was now "shouting" at her to stop doing something that she hated. Shortly afterward Debbie was signed off on sick leave.

Fortunately Debbie had taken the first step by coming to the class. Once she acknowledged that she was blocking her own path to health, wealth, and happiness, Debbie then found the courage to tell her husband. To her surprise he was 100 percent supportive of her desire to leave work. He wanted a happy and healthy wife.

Debbie used the classes to find out what she really wanted to do. She rediscovered her love of writing and has already taken action, putting pen to paper to write her first screenplay. The last I heard, Debbie was quitting work with a $75,000 leaving package.

Do What You Say You're Going to Do

By honoring your truth, you honor yourself. By doing what you say you're going to do, you start to trust your own word. You start to trust yourself. You get more and more in touch with what you want and you start to trust that your heart's desires are OK, irrespective of what others may be thinking. In honoring your own word, you effectively give yourself a massive dose of self-esteem.

Now you are radiating like those who truly respect themselves. Consciously or unconsciously, people will be drawn to you for your magnetic self-confidence. You will attract opportunities from people of integrity. Now that you truly value yourself, others will value you, and you will naturally become a Money Magnet.

Case Study: Helen's Story

Helen changed her thinking to stay focused and connected. Here's her story in her own words:

From a young age, I remember my mum and grandmother saying to me, "We never win anything in this family." That sentence stayed with me throughout my childhood and through many of my adult years. I did not question it, as I thought that was my destiny.

All that changed when I began my coaching journey in 2005. I became exposed to new and more inspiring ways of thinking. All of a sudden I became fed up of settling for second best and I decided to make a conscious intention to become more successful, like many of the people I had read about. I started using intentions to find car parking spaces and—lo and behold—whenever I'd go into a car park, there would be a space waiting for me. Then a few days later, I saw a competition in a magazine to win $1,500 of store *vouchers. All it required was to complete a slogan. I sent it off. Then I got a message back saying that I'd won!*

Being encouraged by this, I then decided to focus on what I really wanted. I was at a charity lunch and one of the prizes there was a beautiful $450 watch. Before the lunch started I was looking at the prizes and imagining myself wearing it. When my name got picked out of the hat, I felt as though I had fulfilled my goal.

Two other great wins have happened since then—a $37,500 package at Stockport County Football Club and a course of singing lessons with celebrated singing coach David Gregory.

When I think about how all these things have happened, I would say that the way I achieved them was first to focus on them and then to take action. The focusing is the lever that makes you take the action to win.

Mirror Magnets

If you have people in your life who are always moaning or who feel that they have been treated badly, whatever you do, do not try to change them. These people are extremely helpful to you in your quest to become a Money Magnet and to stay on track. Why? Because energetically they are there as a reflection of the parts of you that you've not yet acknowledged. When you are working on changing your thoughts to become a Money Magnet, this can be really useful.

Remember, "Like attracts like" and there is no exception. Once you acknowledge where you are still moaning, or where you feel that you have been treated badly, the energies will change. When you shift to a more positive energy, one of three things is likely to happen regarding the negative person in your life:

- The other person will change their behavior.

- They will move away from you.

- You will simply no longer be affected by that aspect of the person.

If you have a few "needy" or "stingy" friends, look to see where you are "needy" or "stingy" yourself. Don't just ditch these friends, as you will only attract more of the same kind until you acknowledge those parts of you.

When you are surrounded by positive, happy, wealthy people, you will know that you're on the right track.

The money is already there. The only thing preventing you from being rich is *you*.

DAY 21

Once a Money Magnet, Always a Money Magnet!

The science is proven. We are energetic beings, and we attract what we think about. Your life is a reflection of your thoughts, both conscious and unconscious. Change your thoughts and you change your life. Adopt Money Magnet habits and you will become a Money Magnet for life. This is your goal and our final topic.

You decided to become a Money Magnet when you committed to reading this book in its entirety. You are making it happen when you apply the exercises and instructions in the book. If you want to increase the amount of money in your life, you want to start thinking differently and you want to start changing your habits.

Be Happy

Being happy is a decision. In every moment of the day, you can choose to be happy. When you choose to be happy, you will feel good and you will attract good things. It makes sense. So why are we all so miserable? It is only a habit. It's now time to break that habit.

Exercise: Get Happy!

Practice smiling, at least eight times a day. Say "Hello" to strangers, with a smile. Look for something beautiful and smile when you discover it. Keep your head up high. Complete your top three priorities each day. Take time out to play. Be silly. Do something that makes someone else happy. Do something that you've always wanted to do. Remember a moment when you were filled with joy. Find something that makes you laugh. Be with happy people.

Mix with Other Money Magnets

It is important to surround yourself with other like-minded people. Do you know that you are the energetic equivalent of the five people you spend most of your time with? What do the people around you say about you? Do they lift your spirits when they enter the room? Can they easily see the positive in most situations? Are they following their heart's desires and living lives packed with passion?

Look out for networks or meetings of like-minded people.

Stay Grateful

A while ago I was introduced to the HeartMath© system. It monitors the electromagnetic rhythms of your heart. Fascinated, I allowed myself to be hooked up to the monitor and I watched as the screen showed a very erratic pulsing line. "Now relax," I was told, "and we'll see if we can slow down your energies to achieve a more relaxed pulse." I relaxed… and nothing happened. My heart energies still appeared "all over the place" despite my relaxed state. "Try being grateful" came the suggestion.

Understanding how important it is to be connected to our hearts, I was eager to be able to calm mine down. As soon as I started to think "grateful thoughts," I watched as the line on the screen reached a steady pulse. It was incredible.

It made sense of all the teachings that I'd read about: gratitude has incredible power.

Gratitude is the key to attracting our heart's wishes. If you are feeling grateful, you will attract more things for which to be grateful.

Writing down what makes you feel grateful is an excellent idea. I can strongly recommend the exercise of writing a minimum of five things in a special "gratitude" journal each night before you go to sleep. Just imagine how your mind will get to work on attracting more for you while you sleep! It's a lovely way to end any day.

Here's a checklist that summarizes what it means to be a Money Magnet! I'd now like you to read through it and see how many statements you can agree with.

The Habits and Thoughts of a Money Magnet

- You love and respect yourself.

- You value what you offer in return for money.

- You respect money by knowing how much you have.

- You respect money by spending it wisely.

- You can talk about money easily and in an appropriate way.

- You sleep well at night knowing that you are financially secure.

- You have time for yourself.

- You enjoy what you do.

- You are happy most of the time.

- You share your happiness with others.

- You have a clear vision of what you desire in the future.

- You experience your vision daily.

- You look at inspiring images every day in your home or office.

- You make a clear intention when you want something.

- You celebrate the riches already in your life.

- You are naturally generous.

- You compliment others and receive compliments easily.

- You stay on top of your clutter—in your home, office, body, and mind.

- You take responsibility, knowing that thoughts attract things to you.

- You maintain a daily focus on what is important to you.

- You take action on any inspiration received.

- You believe in yourself.

- You relax regularly to let go of all the mental clutter.

- You take regular vacations.

- You enjoy a healthy work-life balance.

Now, congratulate yourself on how far you have come since you set out to become a Money Magnet!

Remember, by finding your heart's desire, you can follow your path and let others benefit from the true value you have to give to the world. And in giving value, you will receive value. In feeling worthy, you will be blessed with worthy abundance.

The money is already there. The only thing preventing you from being rich is *you*.

Afterword

Each person has their own journey. The steps outlined in this book have worked for hundreds of my students, and I have witnessed some amazing financial breakthroughs as a result of the "How to Become a Money Magnet!" workshops.

Once you set an intention, you set in motion the attraction of that possibility. You are then likely to attract people and opportunities to support you in reaching your desired reality. Follow your intuition and explore every opportunity that comes your way. It could be a business opportunity, a friend's advice, or a particular therapy.

Sometimes it's difficult to point to the one thing that will make you a Money Magnet. More often it will involve a number of steps and points of clarity along a winding road, before you emerge triumphant.

Follow the steps in this book to attract money regularly. Here's a summary:

- Understand how your thoughts dictate the quality of your life.

- Be clear and specific on how much money you wish to attract.

- Make friends with money and understand your current financial situation.

- Break your existing pattern toward money.

- Start expecting to receive more money.

- Become rich in your imagination, your language, and your actions.

- Clear space for more money.

- Follow your passion and you will attract money.

- Act on all opportunities that come your way.

- Stay connected to your truth and you'll stay connected to abundance.

In Feng Shui the human being is the connection between heaven and earth. The heart is the connecting point within the human. The tricky bit, of course, is staying connected!

You live in an abundant universe, and you were born to live an abundant life. You are unique. You are powerful. It's time to celebrate the wonder of life and the wonder of you. It's time to look to your true self, and to cut through the cloud of limiting thoughts and low self-worth. Then you can be the magnificent magnet that you were born to be.

The money is already there. The only thing preventing you from being rich is *you*.

About the Author

Marie-Claire Carlyle is a Feng Shui consultant and transformational coach, coaching individuals and corporate clients, and inspiring audiences with her passion.

CONNECT WITH
HAY HOUSE
ONLINE

🌐 hayhouse.co.uk **f** @hayhouse

📷 @hayhouseuk 🐦 @hayhouseuk

▶️ @hayhouseuk ♪ @hayhouseuk

Find out all about our latest books & card decks • Be the first to know about exclusive discounts • Interact with our authors in live broadcasts • Celebrate the cycle of the seasons with us • Watch free videos from your favourite authors • Connect with like-minded souls

'The gateways to wisdom and knowledge are always open.'

Louise Hay